God's Love Story

God's Love Story

A CANONICAL TELLING

Joshua Joel Spoelstra

WIPF & STOCK · Eugene, Oregon

GOD'S LOVE STORY
A Canonical Telling

Copyright © 2020 Joshua Joel Spoelstra. All rights reserved. Except for brief quotations in critical publications or reviews, no part of this book may be reproduced in any manner without prior written permission from the publisher. Write: Permissions, Wipf and Stock Publishers, 199 W. 8th Ave., Suite 3, Eugene, OR 97401.

Wipf & Stock
An Imprint of Wipf and Stock Publishers
199 W. 8th Ave., Suite 3
Eugene, OR 97401

www.wipfandstock.com

PAPERBACK ISBN: 978-1-7252-5772-6
HARDCOVER ISBN: 978-1-7252-5773-3
EBOOK ISBN: 978-1-7252-5774-0

Manufactured in the U.S.A. FEBRUARY 6, 2020

To Julie
(Proverbs 18:22; 31:10)

Contents

Introduction xi
  Thesis and Scope xi
  Methodology xiii
  Qualifications xvii

1 Betrothal 1
  1.1 Betrothal, the Concept 1
  1.2 God Calling and Wooing 2
  1.3 Abrahamic Promises; or, the Engagement Ring 3
  1.4 Patriarchal Promises; or, the Heirloom/Promise Ring 6
  1.5 A Very Long Betrothal: Timing and Tensions 8
  1.6 Warding Off Potential Suitors (Gods) 11

Excursus A: Bride-Price 18

2 Marriage 22
  2.1 Covenant as Marriage 22
  2.2 Eloping(?) to the Wedding Chapel 23
  2.3 The Wedding Ceremony 24
  2.4 Covenant Faithfulness as Obedience to the Law of the LORD 31
  2.5 Homemaking: Entering and Settling the Promised Land 34

Excursus B: Vow (or Covenant) Renewal Ceremony 37

3 Unfaithfulness 44
  3.1 Covenant Unfaithfulness as Spiritual Adultery 44
  3.2 The Golden Calf Affair 45

Contents

  3.3 A Second Ceremony 48
  3.4 A (Near) Continual Affair 49
  3.5 Spiritual Adultery in Hosea and Ezekiel 51
  3.6 Fertility Cults 54
  3.7 God Vies for Israel's Affection 56

Excursus C: Risk of Relationship 61

4 Divorce 64
  4.1 Divorce, the Problematic Concept 64
  4.2 Marital Tensions: The Unfaithfulness of the Israelites and the Faithfulness of God 66
  4.3 Annulling the Marriage 68
  4.4 Separation and Estrangement 70
  4.5 Hopes for Reconciliation 74
  4.6 Trying to Observe a Broken Covenant, or Participate in an Annulled Marriage? 77

Excursus D: Ring Off—Ring On 79

5 (Re)Marriage 84
  5.1 Marriage (Again) 84
  5.2 A New Covenant 85
  5.3 Free to Remarry? 92
  5.4 Jesus as Bridegroom and the Church as Bride 92
  5.5 The New Jerusalem as the Bride of Christ 95
  5.6 The Eternal Wedding Banquet 96
  5.7 Wedding Invitations 101

Excursus E: Wife-at-the-Well Type-Scene 102

Conclusion 105
  Summary 105
  Implications 110
Bibliography 113

Acknowledgments

THE GENESIS AND EVOLUTION of this book has been long and diverse. Initially, it was presented at a youth camp in Wisconsin (2006), and then at a college retreat in Oregon (2008). Next, I expanded it for a sermon series in my first pastorate in Idaho (2010). Later, it served as one lens through which I taught Old Testament Survey at a university in South Carolina (2016–2019). To each audience, I am grateful for your attention, engagement, and feedback—it has polished my canonical telling of God's Love Story as is now published.

Abbreviations

ABD	David Noel Freedman, ed. *Anchor Bible Dictionary*. 6 vols. New York: Doubleday, 1992.
BCE	Before Common Era
BDB	Brown, Francis, S. R. Driver, and Charles A. Briggs. *Hebrew and English Lexicon of the Old Testament, with an Appendix Containing the Biblical Aramaic*. Peabody: Hendrickson, 2006.
HALOT	Koehler, Ludwig, and Walter Baumgartner. *The Hebrew and Aramaic Lexicon of the Old Testament*. 2 vols. London: Brill, 2001.
TDNT	Gerhard Kittel, ed. *Theological Dictionary of the New Testament*. 10 vols. Grand Rapids: Eerdmans, 1964.

Introduction

Thesis and Scope

SINCE GOD IS LOVE (1 John 4:8, 16) and, as the author of life and salvation (cf. Acts 3:15; Heb 12:2), reveals the whole of history (Gen 1–2; Rev 21:16; 22:13; cf. Job 26; Ps 8; Rom 1), then it can be deduced that one primary lens through which to read the metanarrative of Scripture is a love story. Indeed, from Old Testament to New Testament, from Genesis to Revelation, from the beginning of time unto eternity, God has chosen to reveal God's plan of redemption and salvation through the metaphorical means of a love story. God creates from a place of love; and God is the one who initiates loving, fulfilling relationship with humanity.[1]

As with every love relationship, God's love story involving humanity has several dynamic phases; and, just like every love relationship, God's love story comprises both seasons of ecstasy and moments of misery. Within this metaphorical love story telling, the five chapters herein represent the five major developments of God's love story in the Bible: Betrothal, Marriage, Unfaithfulness, Divorce, and (Re)Marriage. Further, the relational evolution between God and God's spouse is largely linear (i.e., historical), facilitating a canonical reading and telling (see further below).

First, in the betrothal stage of God's love story, we see God calling and wooing a people into special relationship; God makes promises to this people, the Hebrews, and delivers on those

---

1. Cf. Henriksen, "God Revealed through Human Agency," 453–72.

INTRODUCTION

promises, proving to be an exemplary suitor over against other gods. Second, in the marriage phase of God's love story, the wedding ceremony between God and the Israelites is set at Mt. Sinai as the venue and the Mosaic Covenant as that marital contract; mutual commitments are made and plans are undertaken for the newlyweds' future, so to speak. Third, in the extended unfaithfulness segment, God's covenant partner (bride) chases after the alleged benefits (pleasures) of other gods (lovers) ; the elongated covenant disobedience (marital unfaithfulness) that Israel commits compromises the integrity of the marital relationship with God. Fourth, in the divorce period, this metaphorical expression in the prophets explains the exile, God's expulsion of the Israelites from the land (home); an estrangement sets in between God and the Israelites, by means of said covenantal punishment, yet even still there is hope of reconciliation based on the gracious restoration of God. Fifth, in the (re)marriage phase of God's love story, God—in Jesus—not only takes back people of Jewish decent but also Gentiles for a(nother) marriage or (new) covenant; this covenant of redemption and salvation is eternal in its duration and is based on grace through faith in Jesus as Messiah/Christ and Savior. These abovementioned movements of God's love story are portrayed in Scripture in both literal and nonliteral senses (see further below), which enriches the overall message of the Bible.

In addition, after each chapter of the five stages of God's love story, I will present various excursive discussions on associated subtopics. Like the main body of the present work, these too will focus on stages, phases, and aspects of the Divine love story; these five shorter excursuses are also canonical in scope and method. The auxiliary treatments are bracketed off from the main chapters for a couple reasons; first, to not detract from the dominant theme of the main body (chapters), and, second, to add supplementary information to the conversation, substantiating the total presentation.

"Excursus A" is correlated to chapter 1, "Betrothal," as it explores the biblical tradition and examples of the bride-price, which is deposited into the marriage as a resource and an expression of

Introduction

the bride's value. "Excursus B" relates to chapter 2, "Marriage," in that it traces a figurative vow renewal ceremony (or literal covenant renewal ceremony) to show the (generational) longevity of the Israelites' commitment to their faithful God. "Excursus C" interacts with chapter 3, "Unfaithfulness," by taking a broader look at the tremendous risk of heartbreak and fractured union that God undertakes in pursuing intimate relationship with humankind. "Excursus D" is associated with chapter 4, "Divorce," as it sketches the figurative imagery of God removing God's metaphoric wedding ring, and the literal import that that gesture signifies in terms of the Davidic dynasty and the overall commitment between God and the Israelites as God later reapplies the same ring. "Excursus E" is connected to chapter 5, "(Re)Marriage," insofar as it investigates the biblical type-scene, in which a man meets his bride-to-be at a well and eventually enjoys the bliss of marital union. In each of these excursuses, furthermore, the love story themes culminate in Jesus and open new dimensions of salvation-relationship.

Methodology

There are a few interpretive methodologies which must be registered, so that the exegetical integrity of the investigation is ensured to proceed upon solid footing. In short, this book canonically engages the metaphor of God's love story, specifically through the vehicle of biblical covenants. The three major methodological underpinnings, therefore, are canonical criticism, metaphorical studies, and covenant theology.

Canonical Criticism

The canon of the Bible refers to the scope of the Old and New Testaments. "Canonical criticism demands that Scripture be viewed as a unified, organic entity," explicates Eryl Davies, "and it requires the reader to respect the overarching perspective and character of

INTRODUCTION

the tradition in its entirety."[2] Much has been written on this interpretive approach of the Christian Bible,[3] that is valuing the unity and cohesive message of God's creative acts and redemptive movements in the Old and New Testaments. Thus, God's love story will be appreciated in its fullness as the whole of the canon of Scripture is engaged; indeed, from Genesis to Revelation God is committed to revealing the heart of God as well as revealing the contour of redemptive history through many meaningful metaphors, notwithstanding a dramatic love story.

A canonical scope, furthermore, traces the full arc of God's redemptive history; and this full arch is how this book differs from others similar to it. God's love story as a metaphor that stretches much of the Bible is not a new idea, and several have written on the subject; however, what has been written previously—and as excellent as these volumes are—are partial treatises, spanning part of the canon and/or are focused on a few aspects of God's love story.[4] Consequently, there is a need for an all-encompassing treatment of God's love story where the entire Bible is (representatively) covered, surveying all the main moves and robust intricacies of relationship between God and God's people.

Metaphorical Studies

While literal, nonfigurative biblical literature is dedicated to love and sexuality in the Bible—chiefly, Song of Songs (which is outside the scope of the present work)[5]—the metaphorical, metanarrative

---

2. Davies, *Biblical Criticism*, 115 (see also 114–20). Furthermore, "Canonical criticism serves as a salutary reminder that texts can prove mutually illuminating, and that inter-textual dialogue can often help the reader penetrate the deeper significance of a particular passage and appreciate its fuller implications" (Davies, *Biblical Criticism*, 120).

3. Childs, *Introduction to the Old Testament as Scripture*; Sanders, *Canon and Community*. See also Rendtorff, *Canonical Hebrew Bible*.

4. See, e.g., Smolarz, *Covenant and the Metaphor of Divine Marriage*; Pitre, *Jesus the Bridegroom*.

5. There is much controversy regarding the interpretation of Song of Songs, on the one hand (namely, whether it is literal or allegory), and, on the other

INTRODUCTION

love story is the objective of the present work. Metaphorical studies of biblical literature is an increasing field of biblical scholarship.[6] Regarding the nature of metaphor and its use in the Bible, Shimon Bar-Efrat elucidates:

> The word [metaphor] is used in a non-literal sense, there being similarity but no direct continuity between its literal and non-literal meanings, and the things which the word indicates in its literal and non-literal meanings belong to completely different and separate spheres. In many cases one sphere is abstract or spiritual while the other is concrete.... The value of metaphors is that they are able to carry and transfer considerable emotional charge or illuminate something in a new (and sometimes surprising) way, often achieving a concrete representation or a vivid image.[7]

Such is the aim of God's redemptive history through the metaphorical vehicle of a love story—to convey literal events and actions with the emotionality of the best and worst parts of a love story, so that the serenity and severity of that relationship is underscored. The interplay between literal and metaphorical can be imaged as representing the two sides of a coin, generally speaking; throughout this book, the one concept (e.g., metaphorical) will be referred to as the *counterpart* of the other (e.g., literal) as both are juxtaposed.[8]

The interrelationship of the literal and nonliteral stages in God's love story is well-defined in the following table.

---

hand, considerable interaction with ancient Near Eastern poetry and artefacts pertaining to enchantment and the spells of love and lovemaking that would detract too far from our current interest and pursuits.

6. For examples of interpretation of biblical metaphors, see Stienstra, *YHWH Is the Husband of His People*; Weiss, *Figurative Language in Biblical Prose*; Jindo, *Biblical Metaphor Reconsidered*; Tilford, *Sensing World, Sensing Wisdom*.

7. Bar-Efrat, *Narrative Art in the Bible*, 209.

8. The term *figurative* is also be used throughout this book. While there is some semantic overlap between figurative language and metaphor, they are not one and the same. See e.g., Glucksberg, *Understanding Figurative Language*.

INTRODUCTION

God's Love Story	
Metaphorical	**Literal**
Betrothal	Calling of, and Promises to Abraham, Patriarchs
Marriage	Faithfulness to the Mosaic/Sinaitic Covenant
Unfaithfulness	Israel's Covenantal Disobedience
Divorce	Exile (Covenantal Curse) of Israel and Judah
(Re)Marriage	New Covenant; Jesus' Salvation

Much more detail and nuance are expounded in each respective chapter, but this is a passable synopsis.

Covenant Theology

The metaphorical, canonical telling of God's love story hinges upon the concept of covenant. Making and entering covenant, keeping and guarding covenant, violating and breaking covenant, etc., are all developments in the love story between God and God's spouse, i.e., covenant people. Therefore, covenant theology, in an approximate form, undergirds the present work.[9]

Reformed in origin and nature, covenant theology grapples with the correlation between Law and Gospel, that is between various merit-based covenants in the Old Testament and the grace-based covenant of the New Testament.[10] The covenants in the Old Testament are the Noachian (Gen 9), Abrahamic (Gen 15, 17), Mosaic/Sinaitic (Exod 19–24), Davidic (2 Sam 7), and some also postulate a creation covenant (Gen 1–2). In their own ways, these covenants all foreshadow and are fulfilled by Jesus in the new covenant.

While this is an enormously complex subject, the present volume, with its love story theme, selectively interacts with a few covenants as they compound upon each other in nature and scope

---

9. See, e.g., Dumbrell, *Covenant and Creation*; Horton, *Introducing Covenant Theology*; LaRondelle, *Our Creator Redeemer*. See also Kline, *Kingdom Prologue*.

10. Cf. Fuller, *Gospel and Law*.

INTRODUCTION

throughout redemptive history. Specifically, God's covenant(s) with Abraham in terms of land and descendants (Gen 15, 17) and God's covenant with the Israelites of being a liberated society (Exod 19–24) are fleshed out throughout this book to the extent necessary in fulfilling the thesis that the overarching biblical message is God's love story, as viewed through a metaphorical lens. I therefore acknowledge both the separateness of each covenant and their relatability one to another and am conscientious of the covenant confusion fallacy; nevertheless, the canonical and metaphorical methodologies effect the fluidity between the covenants in the present telling.[11]

Qualifications

This book is designed to be a semi-academic/semi-popular volume; accordingly, the body of the text is accessible to a wide readership, while technical discussions and citations are relegated to the footnotes. This volume could have been lengthier than what it is; however, I have opted for brevity so that the love story theme is distilled into a clear, precise portrait, whereas protracted discussion would have invariably diluted the love story metaphor.

The following treatise is primarily theological and not practical in purpose. While I validate the seriousness and significance of pragmatic quandaries, many other books have been written toward that end. Rather, my goal is to present God's love story involving humanity as portrayed in the Bible, particularly God's covenantal partner or potential covenantal partner(s), to give acclaim to God and God's beautiful purposes. Of course, some practical issues may be inferred from the theological presentation, though I will leave it to you, the reader, to so extrapolate application; notwithstanding, at the end of the book (conclusion) some integrative implications are briefly drawn.

One last item I would like to register is a note on gender neutrality. While I absolutely value gender-neutral language as it

11. In this way, I do implicitly employ a reader-response methodology, too; see Davies, *Biblical Criticism*, 17–39.

xvii

INTRODUCTION

relates to God in the Bible, and though I use gender-neutral language of God as much as possible, there will still be times when I refer to God in the masculine and Israel in the feminine. This is done because the Bible was crafted in a patriarchal society and such is its outlook; further, since the norm of a heterosexual relationship underlies the biblical corpora, it is resultant to—as Scripture does—speak figuratively of God as the husband and Israel/Christians as the wife in covenantal/marriage relationship(s).

Upon this orientation, it is now time to get swept up into God's love story.

1

Betrothal

1.1 Betrothal, the Concept

BETROTHAL IS A BIT of an antiquated word, but I use it intentionally. To speak of God's pursuit of a people for covenant (marriage) relationship, I wish to avoid the improprieties of terms such as *dating, seeing,* or *hanging out* because of their libidinous connotations. Rather, with the word *betrothal* I wish to convey the decencies and valor of God in God's pursuit of special relationship.

In this chapter the betrothal period is plotted, its duration and development. The time frame for this betrothal is approximately seven hundred years, stretching from Gen 12, the call of Abra(ha)m,[1] through Exod 19, the giving of the Mosaic/Sinaitic Covenant.[2] The betrothal period between God and the Hebrew people is extremely long in human terms; although, when

---

1. While Abram's name is changed to Abraham in Gen 17:5, *Abraham* will be used throughout for sake of convenience and consistency; likewise, *Sarah* will be used in all cases for convenience and consistency, though she is *Sarai* at times.

2. That the total betrothal period (Gen 12:1–3 to Exod 19) is roughly 700 years takes into consideration the life spans of the patriarchs (specially, how old each was when their heir was born), including Joseph, and the four-hundred-year period in Egypt (Gen 15:13; Acts 7:6; cf. 430 years in Exod 12:40; Gal 3:17).

considering an infinite God, not bound by time, and the continuous (i.e., generational) existence of the Hebrew people,[3] the timeline is not too exorbitant. Therefore, the phases of God's betrothal with a chosen people include calling and wooing, generational promising of a long-term relationship along with the acknowledgment of its benefits, and even how God wards off potential suitors.

1.2 God Calling and Wooing

Starting the love story at Gen 12, and glossing over Gen 1–11, is deliberate for a few reasons. Genesis 1–11 is universal in scope, with a view of all humanity and primordial events, while Gen 12 and following has one family in focus. Initially, Gen 1–11 sees God's high level of involvement with the created order, imminently present and involved in human and world affairs; however, God ostensibly becomes gradually more distant and removed in the latter part of Gen 1–11. Whereas before the flood God walks with Adam, Eve, and Enoch and speaks directly with the first parents, Cain, and Noah, after the flood God remotely intervenes in events, like the Tower of Babel, and does not directly speak with humans. With such a trajectory of waning involvement and revelation over many generations, God's sudden call of Abraham in Gen 12 is poignantly marked; God then personally reveals Godself and periodically converses with (members of) a family, a chosen people.

Relationship, romantic or otherwise, is always catalyzed by an active, intentional initiative. God initiates relationship with Abraham when God speaks to him, inviting Abraham to follow the leading of God unto a new life.

> The LORD said to Abram, 'Go from your country and your kindred and your father's house to the land that I

---

3. The first person called a *Hebrew*, in Scripture, is Abram (Gen 14:13); thence, Joseph is referred to as a Hebrew (Gen 39:14, 17; 41:12). Once the Hebrew people proliferate in Egypt (cf. Exod 1:15–16, 19; 2:7, 11, 13), the term *Israelites* becomes the favorable term in the Old Testament for the chosen people of God (cf. the anachronistic, editorial instances of *Israelites* before Exodus in Gen 32:32; 36:31; 46:8; 50:25).

will show you. I will make of you a great nation, and I will bless you, and make your name great, so that you will be a blessing. I will bless those who bless you, and the one who curses you I will curse; and in you all the families of the earth shall be blessed." (Gen 12:1–3 NRSV)

In Gen 12:1–3 God makes three promises to Abraham, which he can expect in this relationship with God: land, descendants, and blessings. Abraham indeed responds to God's invitation of a betrothal by enacting the primary injunctions: following God's leading and direction. Abraham's extended family had previously left their homeland of Ur of the Chaldeans and migrated as far as Haran (Gen 11:31); this is essentially moving from the western most part of the fertile crescent to the northern most point. From there, Abraham and Sarah (along with nephew Lot and his wife) respond to God's call and leave their father's household to arrive at the land of Canaan (Gen 15:4–7; cf. Gen 11:31); Canaan is the western- (though not southern-) most point of the fertile crescent.

Abraham traveled a long distance in order to go begin the betrothal relationship with God; nevertheless, when Abraham finally got to his destination "the LORD appeared to Abram," reiterating the divine promises (Gen 12:7 NRSV). Both in Shechem and East Bethel Abraham builds an altar, which serves as a commemoration and an open channel for direct communication with God (Gen 12:7–8; cf. Gen 13:4, 18). The establishment of trust and communication while learning about each other are marks of a good, healthy relational foundation; and this is present with God and Abraham.

1.3 Abrahamic Promises; or, the Engagement Ring

The engagement ring is a familiar custom in many cultures; it signifies a commitment between two persons who will invariably become married. At the wedding ceremony, the engagement ring is joined by an accompanying band when marriage vows are spoken to one another before witnesses, resulting in the formalizing of the marriage. The marriage band is typically less ornate than the engagement ring, for it confirms the relationship already in place. Figuratively, there is an equivalent with God and the Hebrew ancestors.

Throughout Abraham's life God reiterates those original betrothal promises to him (Gen 12:1–3)—and God even bolsters the unequivocal nature of the commitment by making more robust gestures. God effectively formalizes each of the three promises into covenants. A covenant is a solemn oath made between two parties with irreversible, legal terms. In the love story perspective, the covenants with Abraham may be viewed as a metaphorical engagement ring. The promise of land formalizes into a covenant in Gen 15, the promise of descendants formalizes into a covenant in Gen 17, and even the promise of blessing essentially formalizes into a covenant in Gen 14. Each promise turn covenant will briefly be developed in turn, yet the different types of covenants must first be registered.

There are mainly two types of ancient Near Eastern covenants which are attested in the Old Testament. One type of covenant is unilateral; here one party promises to do something irrespective of the other party's involvement and/or cooperation. Another kind of covenant is bilateral; contractual in nature, both parties must uphold and be accountable to the terms of the compact. Additionally, biblical covenants are always comprised of a promise and a sign; the covenantal promise is the term and the covenantal sign is the visible representation that the covenant is being upheld and maintained.[4] These definitions and qualifications provide a framework in understanding the nature of God's covenants with Abraham for the generations to follow.

God's promise to Abraham of land formalizes into a covenant in Gen 15. There "the LORD made a covenant with Abram, saying, 'To your descendants I give this land, from the river of Egypt to the great river, the river Euphrates . . .'" (Gen 15:18[–21] NRSV).

---

4. Before Abraham, an example of a covenant is the so-called Noachian Covenant, where God's unilateral covenantal promise is that never again will the world be destroy by means of a flood and the covenantal sign accompanying that promise is the presence or appearance of the (rain)bow in the sky (Gen 9:1–17).

Betrothal

This is the covenantal promise; and the covenantal sign would be, by inference, Abraham's descendants settled in and occupying the land of Canaan at some future date (Gen 15:13–16). This covenant is unilateral, moreover, by virtue of what transpires at the covenant ratifying ceremony. Rather than God and Abraham passing through the split animal halves (Gen 15:8–10), as is standard for two parties to do (cf. Jer 34:18–19), God induces a deep sleep to fall upon Abraham at the crucial moment (Gen 15:12); instead, two manifestations of God, a smoking firepot and flaming torch, pass through the pieces of animals (Gen 15:17), meaning that God represents both covenantal parties. Thus, it is entirely upon God to keep the terms of this covenant regarding land—it is a unilateral promise, with the human party not needing to do anything by way of covenantal obligation to obtain a homeland for the Hebrews. This covenant of land can figuratively be seen as God's way of purchasing a house, signing closing papers ahead of the marriage ceremony.

God's promise to Abraham of descendants formalizes into a covenant in Gen 17. If the promise of land is like purchasing a home for the happy couple to live in, the covenant of descendants is like the promise of having children—two major topics that couples must figure out in their relationship: where to live and if/when to have kids. The covenantal promise is that God will make Abraham's descendants innumerable, a great nation (Gen 17:1–8); the covenantal sign is circumcision, that the males be circumcised throughout the generations (Gen 17:9–14). The type of covenant here is somewhat ambiguous, that is whether it is unilateral or bilateral. On the one hand, God is seen as the source of life, granting the ability to procreate and even creating progeny (e.g., Gen 17:15–21; 25:21; 29:31). On the other hand, Abraham and Sarah must engage in sexual congress in order to procreate, which is an active participation toward the goal of the covenant; also, there is the human obligation to perform circumcision for the generations to come. Regardless of the covenant's type, a son is born to Abraham and Sarah, and descendants thence increase exponentially.

God's promise of blessing Abraham and making his family a blessing to other people groups throughout the world essentially—though not technically—formalizes into a covenant in Gen 14. When Abraham encounters Melchizedek, king of (Jeru)Salem and priest of God Most High, Melchizedek "brought out bread and wine" and "blessed him and said, 'Blessed be Abram by God Most High, maker of heaven and earth; and blessed be God Most High, who has delivered your enemies into your hand!' And Abram gave him one-tenth of everything" (Gen 14:18–20 NRSV; cf. Heb 7). That Abraham receives blessing from this messianic-like (i.e., the king-priest hybrid) figure is significant (cf. Ps 110); furthermore, from a New Testament viewpoint, sharing in bread and wine with a messianic figure is evocative of a covenant-making ceremony (Matt 26:26–29 // Mark 14:22–25 // Luke 22:15–20; cf. also Josh 9). Nevertheless, any measure of success, prosperity, or favor is understood to be blessing from God; and, any good suitor wishes to provide the best gifts for one's significant other.

In sum, through the love story metaphorical lens the threefold promise (land, descendants, and blessings) might be figuratively viewed as three engagement rings, or—better—three intertwined bands forming one tripartite engagement ring, by virtue of the covenants associated with the promises.

1.4 Patriarchal Promises; or, the Heirloom/Promise Ring

Sometimes an engagement ring is even precipitated by a promise ring; this ring signifies a promise to become engaged, which in turn will culminate in marriage. A promise ring is often given when the timeline of committed relationship before marriage is extensive. This could be given for various reasons; perhaps both persons are young and want to marry when older, wiser, and more financially secure, or perhaps a promise ring is given in other extenuating circumstances. In the case of Abraham and Sarah and the subsequent patriarchs and matriarchs, the promise ring, engagement ring, and wedding ring serve as a threefold sign of commitment.

Betrothal

In God's betrothal of the Hebrew people, God makes a tripartite promise to Abraham (see again Gen 12:1–3); and this presumes a long-standing, generational commitment which will eventually come to fruition in a marriage-like relationship. Accordingly, this threefold promise is also reiterated to Abraham's son Isaac, and to Isaac's son Jacob; thus, God's compounded promise is extended to three generations of Hebrews in their betrothal (see below).

Occasionally some wedding rings are a family heirloom. Passed down from generation to generation (typically skipping one), the same ring can be enjoyed by more than one wife in a family (usually after being refitted).[5] In a similar fashion, the betrothal promises that God made to Abraham are the very same ones God promises to Abraham's son and grandson. God's tripartite promise of land, descendants, blessings to each patriarch is clearly displayed in the table below.

Abraham	Isaac	Jacob
The LORD said to Abram, "Go from your country and your kindred and your father's house to the <u>land</u> that I will show you. I will make of you a <u>great nation</u>, and I will bless you, and make your name great, so that you will be a <u>blessing</u>. I will bless those who bless you, and the one who curses you I will curse; and in you all the families of the earth shall be blessed." (Gen 12:1–3 NRSV)	The LORD appeared to Isaac and said . . . "I will make your <u>offspring</u> as numerous as the stars of heaven, and will give to your offspring all <u>these lands</u>; and all the nations of the earth shall gain <u>blessing</u> for themselves through your offspring, because Abraham obeyed my voice and kept my charge, my commandments, my statutes, and my laws." (Gen 26:4–5 NRSV)	"I am the LORD, the God of Abraham your father and the God of Isaac; the <u>land</u> on which you lie I will give to you and to your offspring; and your <u>offspring</u> shall be like the dust of the earth, and you shall spread abroad to the west and to the east and to the north and to the south; and all the families of the earth shall be <u>blessed</u> in you and in your offspring." (Gen 28:13–14 NRSV)

---

5. For instance, my wife's wedding ring is an heirloom that I received from my grandmother.

These patriarchal promises are even reiterated to Joseph, who represents the fourth generation; so, the promises of land and descendants (Gen 48:3–20), and blessings (Gen 49:22–26) are again bequeathed. Therefore, on the one hand, this generational promising can be seen as the exact heirloom promise ring getting handed down to each successive generation; on the other hand, this phenomenon can also be seen as the engagement ring remaining a historically present promise for the Hebrew people.

1.5 A Very Long Betrothal: Timing and Tensions

The much-elongated betrothal period of God and the Hebrew people may reasonably seem problematic. As mentioned above (1.1), this time frame is approximately seven hundred years and over the course of multiple generations. What is important to understand, though, is the fact that God is aware of the lengthy interval and has a purpose for it. In short, there is much opportunity for God to make good on God's promises. Timing is everything, and God is coordinating two critical factors simultaneously, throughout the betrothal period, in order to deliver on the threefold betrothal promise.

Regarding the promise of land,

> the LORD [had] said to Abram, "Know this for certain, that your offspring shall be aliens in a land that is not theirs, and shall be slaves there, and they shall be oppressed for four hundred years; but I will bring judgment on the nation that they serve, and afterward they shall come out with great possessions.... And they shall come back here in the fourth generation; for the iniquity of the Amorites is not yet complete." (Gen 15:13–16 NRSV)

In this foretelling, God discloses that Abraham's descendants will migrate away from the land of Canaan for a time yet will later repossess it when the sin of the Amorite people group is fulfilled (cf. Exod 3:7–10, 16–17; 6:2–8); in actuality, one people dispossessing another people of their land is a fairly common means of punishment which God orchestrates.[6] The timing of when to bring the Israelites into the promised land is part and parcel of an issue related to the second betrothal promise: descendants.

Regarding descendants, God is also delivering on this promise—specifically during the period of enslavement of the Hebrew people in Egypt. When in slavery, "the Israelites were fruitful and prolific; they multiplied and grew exceedingly strong, so that the land was filled with them" (Exod 1:7 NRSV; cf. Gen 47:27; Ps 105:24; Acts 7:17); in fact, "the more they were oppressed, the more they multiplied and spread, so that the Egyptians came to dread the Israelites" (Exod 1:12 NRSV). While the circumstances and conditions of the Israelites were horrendous, it was not unforeseen (see again Gen 15); God was fulfilling—even then—the promise of multiplying the descendants of Abraham and Sarah.

A census of the Hebrew descendants before and after four centuries of slavery clearly documents the proliferation. When the Hebrews entered Egypt, they numbered seventy persons (Gen 46:27; Exod 1:5). When the Israelites made their exodus from Egypt, they numbered 603,550 men, twenty years and older (Exod 38:26); one year after the liberation from slavery, the Israelites (again) numbered 603,550 men, though excluding the Levite tribe (Num 1:46–47; 2:32–33). Once wives and children are factored into the count, the estimated figure would be approximately three to five million people. This exponential increase of offspring is a fitting population by which to inhabit the promised land (cf. Exod 23:29–30; Deut 7:22–23).

God's promise of blessings is also not without fulfillment in the betrothal period. Routinely the patriarchs prosper in resources (Gen 12:16–20; 20:14–18; 26:12–14; 31:17–18). Joseph finds favor before Pharaoh and is permitted to establish his extended family in "the best part of the land . . . Goshen" (Gen 47:6 NRSV). Even at their exodus, the Israelites despoil the Egyptians of great possessions (Exod 12:35–36; Ps 105:37), just as God had foretold

---

6. Assyria is God's punishing tool upon Israel (Isa 10:5–7). Babylonia is God's punishing tool upon Judah (Isa 47:6; Jer 20:4). Persia is God's punishing tool upon Babylonia (Jer 25:12; 50:18).

(Gen 15:14); and it is with these resources that the Israelites could construct the ornate tabernacle (Exod 35–40). Consequently, the long betrothal period has its purposes; and, the time finally came for God to bring to convergence the developing elements of land readiness and Israelite proliferation.

The absence of blessings, alternatively, is also present in the betrothal stage of God and Israel's relationship. When the Israelites fall from favor in the sight of the Egyptians and become enslaved, this is a crucial moment where God's damsel is in distress, so to speak, and when God as the knight in shining armor swoops in to save her. The betroths' cry of distress, cry for rescue and God's intervention are vividly captured in the following two passages.

> The Israelites groaned under their slavery, and cried out. Out of the slavery their cry for help rose up to God. God heard their groaning, and God remembered his covenant with Abraham, Isaac, and Jacob. God looked upon the Israelites, and God took notice of them. (Exod 2:23–25 NRSV)

> Then the LORD said, "I have observed the misery of my people who are in Egypt; I have heard their cry on account of their taskmasters. Indeed, I know their sufferings, and I have come down to deliver them from the Egyptians" (Exod 3:7–8a NRSV)

The outcry of Israel ascends to God and God in deliverance descends. Whenever the Bible records God remembering someone or something, this does not mean that God had previously forgotten that person or situation. Instead, this type of statement, i.e., God's remembrance, indicates the catalytic moment of divine intervention.[7]

God's liberation comes at the human agency of Moses and Aaron. For the Hebrew people who had lost faith that God would bring them out into marriage, God takes this opportunity to again woo the Israelites whom God has called into betrothal relationship. God calls and woos again by means of displaying God's

---

7. See Childs, *Memory and Tradition in Israel*, 34. E.g., Gen 8:1; 30:22.

BETROTHAL

omnipotence in Egypt through miraculous signs and wonders, namely the ten plagues.

1.6 Warding Off Potential Suitors (Gods)

A common motif in modern story, typically presented in film, is that of the unlikely couple who come to find they are attracted to each other as they together go through an unsuspected series of events. Usually adventurous, dangerous, or even traumatic in nature, the oddly paired couple experience a shared journey, which, like a crucible, brings them together in a powerful, dramatic, and predictably romantic, way. Examples are too numerous to list; it's plotline formula!

A loose comparison might be made of God and the Israelites in the opening movement of Exodus. God is like the man, the Hebrew people are like the woman; the adventure is getting to Mt. Sinai, and the dangers along the way—which will bring the two together—are chiefly the ten plagues and the exodus event. The ten plagues, further, are not only the dramatic, crucible-like shared experience, but in those plagues God fights for the heart, affections, and loyalty of God's betrothed.

The ten plagues, also, are the crowbar that it takes for God to break the will of Pharaoh and the bondage of slavery unto liberation. In addition, there is another layer of meaning embedded in the plague cycle. God says, "I will pass through the land of Egypt . . . on all the gods of Egypt I will execute judgments: I am the LORD" (Exod 12:12 NRSV; cf. Num 33:4b). So, the primary, or at least theological, reason God sent ten plagues upon Egypt was in order to defeat the popular gods of the Egyptian pantheon. These actions may figuratively be seen as systematically warding off other suitors, other gods; gods or suitors who may have captured Israel's heart (cf. Ezek 23:3, 8, 19–21, 27).

In the dramatic fashion in which the material is presented in Exodus, the seemingly random environmental, agricultural, and astronomical anomalies that are the ten plagues are therefore systematically directed to supplant each false god's power and provision—thereby ascribing supremacy to the LORD God.[8] Indeed, each object or item that is highlighted in the plague cycle represents a main god of the Egyptian pantheon; so God wards off other potential suitors (gods) by upsetting the respective god's or goddess's purported benevolent attributes. When Pharaoh pleads for Moses to ask the LORD God to take the plague away, to make it end, two implicit significances are registered; first, Pharaoh essentially casts off that respective Egyptian god, and second, the LORD God is demonstrated—and effectively confessed—as being more powerful than the Egyptian god and the true source of that god's nature.

What follows, then, is this theological perspective of the love story rival with each respective plague: "On all the gods of Egypt I will execute judgments: I am the LORD" (Exod 12:12 NRSV).[9]

1. Blood

Hapi, the Nile-god, was represented as "a hermaphrodite, capable thus of both fertilizing that land (the male aspect) and also nourishing it (the female aspect)."[10] Additionally, "Osiris is also identified as the god of the Nile since in Egyptian mythology Hapi apparently was his child."[11] By virtue of being associated with the Nile, Osiris was considered the god of agriculture, like Hapi, for by the water source crops rise from the ground; this seasonal growing and harvesting was likened to resurrection, so Osiris was also considered the god of resurrection.[12] Consequently, for the LORD God to turn the Nile water into blood evoked the death of Hapi and Osiris, so cleansing in and irrigating with the Nile is no longer viable. Thus, the LORD God is sovereign over Hapi and Osiris.

---

8. *LORD* (in all caps) is representative of the divine personal name *YHWH* from *I AM* (see Exod 3:14). The designation *LORD God* will be used throughout this section to differentiate between the gods of Egypt and YHWH.

9. Cf. Spero, "'Against All the Gods of Egypt,'" 83–88.

10. Stuart, *Exodus*, 131.

11. Stuart, *Exodus*, 132.

12. See Budge, *Osiris and the Egyptian Resurrection*.

2. Frogs

"Heqet was a frog goddess who helped women to give birth and the dead to be reborn."[13] She "stood for the creation and regeneration of life."[14] The LORD God (in exaggerative humor?) sent a superabundance of frogs which hopped into the palaces, houses, bedrooms, beds, ovens, and kneading bowls (Exod 8:3, 6). The creation explosion or frogs is polemical, in view of Heqet; and the superabundance of dead frogs in the palace, houses, bedroom, bed, ovens and kneading bowls is ironic. Consequently, it is likely the people came to disdain the frog goddess Heqet.

3. Gnats

It is uncertain which Egyptian god the LORD God duels here. But what is noteworthy at this juncture is how the Egyptian magicians could not replicate this plague, as they had the previous couple (Exod 7:22; 8:7; cf. Exod 7:11–12). As a result, "the magicians said to Pharaoh, 'This is the finger of God!'" (Exod 8:19 NRSV). It is provocative that the Egyptian magicians ascribe glory to the LORD God! It takes several more plagues for Pharaoh to so acknowledge the LORD.

4. Flies

To preface, the Hebrew text (the original language of the Old Testament) does not have the word *flies* in it, only *swarm* (Heb. *arov*). The nuance of definition for Heb. *arov* is "noxious insects";[15] this probably correlates to the scarab or dung beetle since they "hatch out of buried dung balls and fly off"[16]—noxious indeed! Khepri, "god of cyclical renewal and of the daily rising and variable aspects

---

13. Pinch, *Handbook of Egyptian Mythology*, 139.
14. Schulz, "Gods of Ancient Egypt," 522.
15. *HALOT*, 1:879.
16. Pinch, *Handbook of Egyptian Mythology*, 152.

of the sun[,] was depicted in the shape of a scarab beetle."[17] It is therefore ironic that a massive swarm of beetles ruined, instead of renewed, the land of Egypt (Exod 8:24); the self-regenerative god was removed by the LORD God (Exod 8:31).[18]

5. Livestock

The LORD God sent pestilence upon the livestock of the Egyptians (but not of the Israelites) with the result that they died. The cow was among the larger livestock, and it was this premiere bovine that represented an Egyptian goddess: Hathor. "She was most commonly shown as a beautiful woman wearing a red solar disk between a pair of cow's horns."[19] Hathor was "the goddess of love and maternity, the protecting deity of birth and regeneration."[20] That the LORD God strikes the livestock dead renders impotent Hathor's ability to source life.

6. Boils

Boils infect the Egyptians (yet not the Israelites) in God's sixth plague; and this appears to be a direct affront to any number of gods or goddesses who were purported to have healing capacities, including Imhotep, Renenutet, and Sekhmet.[21] However, these deities of healing were was not able to provide any relief or healing from the infliction of boils from the LORD God. Like all the other plagues, Pharaoh had to entreat Moses to pray to the LORD God for the removal of the plague.

---

17. Schulz, "Gods of Ancient Egypt," 522.
18. Pinch, *Handbook of Egyptian Mythology*, 152.
19. Pinch, *Handbook of Egyptian Mythology*, 137.
20. Schulz, "Gods of Ancient Egypt," 522.
21. Pinch, *Handbook of Egyptian Mythology*, 148–49, 185–86, 187–88.

BETROTHAL

7. Hail

In the seventh plague, the LORD God hurled down hail and fire from heaven, along with thunder (Exod 9:23). Nut was "the personification of the sky, and represented the feminine principle which was active at the creation of the universe."[22] She was typically represented as "a giant nude woman arched above the earth"[23] and, as such, Nut was supposed to shield her worshipers from any celestial catastrophe. However, the LORD God pierced Nut through with hail and fire, rendering her ineffective.

8. Locusts

The plague of the locust swarm decimated the remaining crops in the land of Egypt. This may be a judgment on the goddess Neith. Neith was "a formidable creator goddess who could be called the Great Mother. . . . The curious symbol that represented Neith in these early times may originally have been a click beetle."[24] Though click beetles are different than locusts, perhaps the superabundance of an insect of proportionate size evinced thought of Neith; regardless, it was clear to Pharaoh's officials at this point that the gods of Egypt were not able to thwart the LORD God's onslaughts (Exod 10:7).

9. Darkness

The most supreme god of the Egyptian pantheon was Ra, or Amun-Re, who is embodied as the sun. "Time began when [Amun-]Rā appeared above the horizon at creation in the form of the Sun, and the life of a man was compared to his daily course."[25] Thus, Amun-Re created himself and was therefore the principle deity of

---

22. Budge, *Egyptian Religion*, 120.
23. Pinch, *Handbook of Egyptian Mythology*, 174.
24. Pinch, *Handbook of Egyptian Mythology*, 169–70.
25. Budge, *Egyptian Religion*, 126.

the pantheon of Egyptian gods, whom he also created.[26] However, for the sun to be blacked out for three days by the LORD God essentially signifies Amun-Re's defeat, even death (however, there was light where the Israelites lived during those three days [Exod 10:23b]).

Another Egyptian deity associated with the sun is Sekhmet, "an aggressive solar goddess who was the instrument of divine retribution."[27] She was considered the pupil or fiery "Eye of Ra."[28] Thus, in the ninth plague, Sekhmet was effectively blinded, and all divine sight or oversight upon Egypt vanished for three days.

10. Firstborn

Even the plague of the death of the firstborn is a means by which the LORD God executed judgment against the gods of Egypt (Exod 12:12; Num 33:4b). The pharaoh was considered a god of the Egyptian pantheon incarnate on earth; thus, Pharaoh's son would become the next god on earth (Egypt).[29] Consequently, when the LORD God struck down the firstborn of Egypt, no power of Pharaoh (god incarnate) could save his son (the next god incarnate).

In sum, the LORD God defeated all these abovementioned gods, just as God promised, "I will pass through the land of Egypt . . . on all the gods of Egypt I will execute judgments: I am the LORD" (Exod 12:12 NRSV). By rivaling other gods, the LORD God contended for the (renewed) affection of the Israelites over against any other loyalty—and the LORD God triumphed. In other (nonmetaphorical) words, the LORD God dissuaded the Israelites from any idolatry (cf. Ezek 23); and, inversely, to promote worshiping the one, true, living God alone.

---

26. Schulz, "Gods of Ancient Egypt," 522.
27. Pinch, *Handbook of Egyptian Mythology*, 187.
28. Pinch, *Handbook of Egyptian Mythology*, 187.
29. See Pinch, *Handbook of Egyptian Mythology*, 100.

BETROTHAL

At this point, i.e., the liberation from enslavement in Egypt upon God's persuasion with and performance of the ten plagues, the love story segues to the next stage: marriage. God has proven to be a faithful and worthy suitor, wooing and winning over the Hebrew people. Choosing each other once again, God and the Israelites will formally enter a marriage-like relationship in the form of entering into covenant together.

Excursus A

Bride-Price

IN THE BETROTHAL STAGE of God's love story (ch. 1), much mention was made of the patriarchs; in this excursus, some of the matriarchs are spotlighted to accentuate the concept of bride-price (cf. Exod 22:16-17), a key (biblical) element in the betrothal period in preparation for marriage. The *bride-price* is a payment of money and/or resources made by the prospective groom's family to the bride's family "to compensate for the bride's services and potential offspring."[1] There are a few instances where the bride-price comes into focus in Genesis, with Rebekah and Leah and Rachel. These biblical narratives will be briefly examined in order to construct a conceptual backdrop by which to understand the significance of the new covenant's/testament's counterpart.

1. Rebekah

When Isaac was forty years old (Gen 25:20), Abraham undertook plans to arrange a marriage for his son. Insistent that Isaac's would-be wife should come from his extended family, Abraham sent his servant to Haran to find her. When the servant of Abraham

---

1. Bar, "What Did the Servant Give," 565. Inversely, a *dowry* is a gift given by the bride's father for the bride upon the wedding; cf. Hamilton, "Marriage (OT and ANE)," *ABD*, 4:561-62.

meets Rebekah at the public well, his prayer for God's guidance in and God's affirmation of identifying the woman whom Isaac is to marry is answered (Gen 24:12–15, 17–21, 23–27). Rebekah is described as "very fair to look upon, a virgin, whom no man had known" (Gen 24:16 NRSV). Realizing that God was granting him success in his assignment, the servant gives Rebekah a nose ring and two arm bracelets of high quality gold (Gen 24:22, 30, 47).[2] In addition, when later meeting her family, Abraham's "servant brought out jewelry of silver and of gold, and garments, and gave them to Rebekah; he also gave to her brother and to her mother costly ornaments" (Gen 24:53 NRSV). These latter items are effectively a bride-price;[3] while the quantity and total value is unknown, this bride-price was evidently an acceptable (perhaps even generous) sum for the family to part with their daughter and sister. In the end, Rebekah consents to marry Isaac (Gen 24:57–58); and after moving to Canaan, Rebekah and Isaac become married (Gen 24:67).

2. Leah and Rachel

Since Jacob had fled for his life from his brother, Esau, he is resourceless when arriving at Haran. As a result, Jacob does not have anything to offer his would-be father-in-law by way of a bride-price when he falls in love with Rachel—who "was graceful and beautiful" (Gen 29:16b NRSV). Nevertheless, Jacob negotiates with Laban in terms of years of labor, and they agree upon seven years as a worthy bride-price.[4] "So Jacob served seven years for

---

2. Westermann (*Genesis 12-36*, 387) rightly notes these items are not a bride-price, instead they are simply presents. Similarly, in the figurative text of Ezek 16, God woos lady Israel by bestowing upon her the following gifts: "I adorned you with ornaments: I put bracelets on your arms, a chain on your neck, a ring on your nose, earrings in your ears, and a beautiful crown upon your head" (Ezek 16:11–12 NRSV; cf. Ezek 23:42). The terminology for nose ring (Heb. *nezem*) and bracelets (Heb. *tsemidim*) is the same as in Gen 24.

3. Cf. Westermann, *Genesis 12-36*, 389. Contra Van Seters, *Abraham in History and Tradition*, 77.

4. See Westermann, *Genesis 12-36*, 466–67; Van Seters, *Abraham in History*

Rachel, and they seemed to him but a few days because of the love he had for her" (Gen 29:20 NRSV).[5]

When the wedding day/week finally came, Laban tricked Jacob and gave him Leah instead. After words were exchanged, Laban gave Rachel to Jacob as his wife in exchange for another seven years of labor (Gen 29:26–30). Thus, in the end, fourteen years of labor was the transactional bride-price for Laban's two daughters (Gen 31:41).[6] From these wives (and handmaids), Jacob/Israel becomes a numerous nation.

3. Christ's Bride

The New Testament champions Jesus of Nazareth as the Son of God, Messiah/Christ, Savior of the world. As such, Jesus is the eternal bridegroom; the bridegroom figure is someone Jesus intimates concerning himself (Matt 9:15 // Mark 2:19–20 // Luke 5:34–35) and is also ascribed to him (John 3:28; Rev 18:23; 19:7–9). While more will be developed on this point in chapter 5 ("[Re]Marriage"), the concept of bride-price as it relates to Jesus is present and poignant.

If Jesus is the bridegroom and the church is the bride of Christ (Eph 5:29–32), then what bride-price has Jesus paid to enter into marriage with her? The New Testament overwhelmingly attests that Jesus gifted nothing less than his very life. Indeed, Jesus has paid the ultimate *price* to purchase—or redeem (cf. Acts 20:28; 1 Pet 1:18–19; Rev 5:19)—his *bride*, the church, the historic collection of those who receive God's salvation by grace through faith in Christ (cf. Rom 10:9–10; Eph 2:4–10).

That Jesus' bride-price is his own life is provocative in a few ways. First, a human life is the most precious of commodities: "No one has greater love than this, to lay down one's life for one's

---

and Tradition, 79–80.

5. By the way, that might be the most romantic verse in the Bible—severe time distortion due to the intensity of love!

6. Perhaps Jacob's six years of working for a portion of Laban's flock is the wives' dowry (cf. Gen 30:25–31:55).

friends" (John 15:13 NRSV). Second, Jesus' *perfect and blameless* life was given for an *imperfect and sinful* (collective) bride; in other words, the church's salvation (bride-price) is the free gift granted by her Savior. Third, if Jesus' bride-price is at the cost and value of his perfect life, then it is upon Jesus' physical resurrection whereupon he enters wedded union with his bride, the church, which is also upon the occurrence of her spiritual resurrection (salvific regeneration). Consequently, the oneness between Savior and saved is the Spirit of Christ, the Holy Spirit of God (John 14, 16; Rom 8:11); the oneness of Jesus and Jesus-disciples (John 15, 17) is a similar phenomenon to the hypostatic union of divine essence and human essence that is Christ incarnate. Through the same vital essence and divine anima, therefore, bridegroom (Christ) and bride (church) share in the same intimate and sacred mystical union (Eph 5:32); and, abiding in Christ (John 15) is portrayed as the zenith of satisfaction of being, the fulfillment of calling and purpose, and the deepest depths of relational contentment.

2

Marriage

2.1 Covenant as Marriage

PRACTICALLY THE ONLY TIME we hear the word *covenant* in North American culture today is in the context of marriage: the marriage covenant. This conceptual terminology is residual from the Bible. Indeed, a covenant may be biblically viewed as a marriage (e.g., Prov 2:17; Mal 2:14–15).[1] As God at one point, specifically, says, in "the covenant that I made with their ancestors" at Mt. Sinai "I took them by the hand to bring them out of the land of Egypt" and "I was their husband, says the LORD" (Jer 31:32 NRSV; cf. also Isa 54:5).

In this chapter, the marriage (metaphoric) or covenant (literal) ceremony between God and the Israelites is presented. This phase in the love story first charts the journey to the wedding venue, and then the events surrounding the ceremony. Within the covenant-making ceremony, attention is given to the marital or covenantal terms and conditions, its vows and ratification. Marriage as the intended and ideal relationship between God and the Hebrew people is also situated in the context of a home, which they aim to enjoy together.

---

1. See Hugenberger, *Marriage as a Covenant*.

MARRIAGE

2.2 Eloping(?) to the Wedding Chapel

Traditionally, when a couple elected to elope to get married it was done under dubious circumstances, namely when parental support for the marriage was absent. In God's love story, while parental support does not fit the metaphor and though the departure of (God and) Israel from Egypt is not done in secret, there are extenuating circumstances which makes for a sudden and swift journey to the place of the marriage ceremony. Further, like elopement, (God and) Israel will not return to the current place of residence (Egypt).

The sudden departure of Israel from Egypt catalyzed during the tenth plague, thence commencing the Israelites' liberation and exodus. The death of the (Egyptian) firstborns took place during the night; accordingly, God instructed the Passover meal to be eaten during nightfall, in preparation for a sudden and speedy departure (Exod 12:11). Interestingly, eloping couples typically steal away at night. While it was morning by the time the Israelites made their exodus (Exod 12:31-36), the eloping concept—that is, a swift journey to a wedding chapel—is still somewhat analogous.

The eloping route was an exceptional journey for the betrothed Hebrew people. Once the Israelites were at the border of Egypt, Pharaoh and his army chased after them in attempts to take them captive again (Exod 14:4-6); however, God protected Israel with an additional miraculous sign and wonder. When the people of God get to the Red Sea, then God caused the sea to be divided thus making water walls on both sides and the ground in the middle dry for God's betrothed to cross through safely. These water walls, however, were recoiled by God when Pharaoh and his armies tried to pass through the opening in the sea, and they drowned. The result of this miraculous and conquering event was such that "the people feared the LORD and believed in the LORD and in his servant Moses" (Exod 14:31b NRSV). Furthermore, the Hebrews respond to their God by breaking out into worship (Exod 15:1-18).[2]

2. The exodus route and sea crossing are contested in biblical scholarship,

Moving along in their eloping journey—in order to get to the wedding chapel and the same mountain that God appeared to Moses, thus delivering on God's promise (Exod 3:12)—God directed their path. "The LORD went in front of them in a pillar of cloud by day, to lead them along the way, and in a pillar of fire by night, to give them light, so that they might travel by day and by night. Neither the pillar of cloud by day nor the pillar of fire by night left its place in front of the people" (Exod 13:21-22 NRSV). God also provided the Israelites with miraculous food and water supply all throughout their trip (Exod 16:15, 31; 17:5b-6). Finally, the Israelites arrived safely at Mt. Sinai after their two-month eloping trip (Exod 19:1), where they then rendezvous with God.

2.3 The Wedding Ceremony

The events at the base of Mt. Sinai (also called Horeb [see, e.g., Exod 3:1; 33:6; Deut 1:2; 4:10]) and the entering of covenant all purport to a marriage ceremony between God and the Israelites. From a metaphorical love story lens, several aspects of the proceedings of the covenant-making ceremony correlate with contemporary wedding ceremonies. Thus, the most analogous elements will be draw out of Exod 19-24.

2.3.1 Preparations

Once at the foot of Mt. Sinai, their wedding chapel, preparations for the marriage ceremony are undertaken. The Israelites had to get their wedding clothes ready for the wedding day, as it were. "The LORD said to Moses: 'Go to the people and consecrate them today and tomorrow. Have them wash their clothes and prepare for the third day, because on the third day the LORD will come down upon Mount Sinai in the sight of all the people'" (Exod 19:10-11 NRSV). And the people did so (Exod 19:14-15). Today, the bridal

---

with many options and alternatives proffered.

party often spends the day leading up to the ceremony primping and preening for the decisive moments.

2.3.2 Processional

Then, after two days of preparation (Exod 19:16a), the wedding ceremony starts. "There was thunder and lightning, as well as a thick cloud on the mountain, and a blast of a trumpet so loud that all the people who were in the camp trembled. Moses brought the people out of the camp to meet God. They took their stand at the foot of the mountain" (Exod 19:16–17 NRSV). Is Moses' escorting the people to God like a father walking his daughter down the aisle? Is being well positioned at the base of the mountain perhaps like standing on the small piece of tape on the raised platform marking the positions of the bridal party? Is the people's trembling like unto nerves during the ceremony? Is the multisensory thunder, lightning, and trumpet blasts loosely reminiscent of wedding bells, processional/recessional music, and the like? The formality and preparations nonetheless indicate the significance of the events.

2.3.3 Consent

Next, the intent to marry and vows are spoken by the LORD God which comprises the Ten Commandments as well as the rest of the law in Exod 20–23. Momentarily, these vows will be expounded (2.3.5); after the marriage vows comes the declaration of intent or commitment—the *I-do*s. The Israelites collectively state their *I-do*s (or *we-will*s) thrice in the marriage ceremony, as seen in the graph below.

The *I-Dos* (or *We-Wills*)		
The people all answered as one: "Everything that the LORD has spoken we will do." Moses reported the words of the people to the LORD. (Exod 19:8 NRSV)	Moses came and told the people all the words of the LORD and all the ordinances; and all the people answered with one voice, and said, "All the words that the LORD has spoken we will do." (Exod 24:3 NRSV)	Then he took the book of the covenant, and read it in the hearing of the people; and they said, "All that the LORD has spoken we will do, and we will be obedient." (Exod 24:7 NRSV)

2.3.4 Certificate

At this juncture, it is time for the signing of the marriage contract. The way that covenants were ratified in ancient Near Eastern cultures most often involved blood. Accordingly, after the third *I-do* (or *we-will*), "Moses took the blood [of a bull] and dashed it on the people, and said, 'See the blood of the covenant that the LORD has made with you in accordance with all these words'" (Exod 24:7–8 NRSV). Now the marriage contract—or covenant—is figuratively signed and notarized.

In North American culture, part of the wedding ceremony pageantry also includes the signing of the marriage certificate by the bride and groom, the minister and witnesses; the photographer typically documents this signing with a picture of the ringed hands of the bride and groom. Whereas modern marriage certificates may be deposited in a safe or mounted in a prominent place, the Israelite's marriage certificate will be secured in the ark of the covenant (Exod 25:16; 1 Kgs 8:9; Heb 9:4); the Israelite's certificate of the marriage contract is, in a different sense, the stone tablets whereupon are written the Ten Commandments.

2.3.5 Vows

To consider the metaphorical marital vows is to focus on the Ten Commandments, mainly. The commitments encapsulated in the

Marriage

Decalogue is the equivalent of the vows "to have and to hold, for richer and poorer, in sickness and in health," etc., which is the ideal for the marriage relationship. The significance of the first three of the Ten Commandments particularly, as wedding vows, address the goal of marital fidelity between the LORD God and the Israelite people. These are as follows: (1) "You shall have no other gods before me" (Exod 20:3 NRSV); (2) "You shall not make for yourself an idol, whether in the form of anything that is in heaven above, or that is on the earth beneath, or that is in the water under the earth" (Exod 20:4 NRSV); (3) "You shall not make wrongful use of the name of the LORD your God, for the LORD will not acquit anyone who misuses his name" (Exod 20:7 NRSV). Each of these marital vows, as it were, deserve elucidation.[3]

1. No Other Gods

Classical wedding vows often include phrases like "forsaking all others" and/or "I pledge thee mine troth [i.e., faithfulness]"; these oaths make fidelity and monogamy the objective. The same is evident in the first (three) commandment(s). "You shall have no other gods before me" means the LORD God is to be Israel's only God (Exod 20:3 NRSV), and this includes no rival idols too (see #2 below). If the Hebrew people only worship the LORD God, then they are forsaking all other gods; but if the Hebrew people worship other gods, then the equivalent of that would be marital infidelity: idolatry. Therefore, the marriage ideal is one of complete faithfulness on the part of God's bride, God's chosen covenant people—and God, as the typified groom, will also to be completely faithful as pledged (Deut 7:9).

---

3. Commandments 5–10 standardize human interaction with one another. Thus, as it is oft said, commandments 1–3 focus on the vertical relationship (i.e., between God and humanity) and commandments 5–10 center on horizontal relationships (i.e., person to person). Regarding commandment 4 (Sabbath day to keep it holy), I see it as a hinge command, joining the vertical and horizontal dimensions; namely, that space and time enfolds human-divine relations.

This first commandment sounds simple enough, yet it was—and is—very countercultural and thus difficult to uphold. As Douglas Stuart explicates:

> Ancient people ... believed in three categories of gods, all of which any individual was likely to differentiate by his or her own beliefs and worship: the personal god, the family god, and the national god. For most Israelites at most times ... Yahweh was merely a national god. Ancient Israelites might have, say, Dagon [the Philistine grain god] (Judg 16:23; 1 Sam 5; 1 Chr 10:10) as their personal god and perhaps Baal [the Canaanite sky god] (e.g., Judg 2:13; 6:25, 28, 30–32; 1 Kgs 16:31–32) as their family god, but they would always have Yahweh as his national God. No Israelite, no matter how totally immersed in idolatry, would ever answer no to the question, "Do you believe in Yahweh?" But most, at most times in Israel's history, would, sadly, see him only as a national god (the one who had brought them out of Egypt or the one to whom they would appeal in times of war).[4]

So, "you shall have no other gods before me" is straightforward, yet it takes an entire lifetime of intentional, relational loyalty to make good on this command/vow to the extent that faith in the LORD God is exclusive. When a covenant people worship, revere, venerate, or even prioritize anything above the LORD God then this command of "no other gods before Me" has been violated. Inversely stated, the first commandment may be worded: Worship the LORD your God alone (cf. Deut 6:4)!

2. No Idols

The second commandment, or wedding vow, which speaks to the Israelites' relationship with God, is: "You shall not make for yourself an idol, whether in the form of anything that is in heaven above, or that is on the earth beneath, or that is in the water under the earth" (Exod 20:4 NRSV). This prohibition is countercultural

---

4. Stuart, *Exodus*, 452.

Marriage

in the face of what was commonplace religious practice in the ancient Near Eastern world, in which Israel was situated. Again, Douglas Stuart elucidates:

> Ancients assumed that the presence of a god or goddess was guaranteed by the presence of an idol since the idol "partook" of the very essence of the divinity it was designed to represent. When, for example, a statue of a given god was carved and certain ritual incantations spoken over that statue to cause the essence of the god to enter it, the statue was then understood to become a functioning conduit for anything done in its presence from the worshiper to that god. In the same way that a modern person might speak to and look into a sound-equipped television camera knowing that their words and actions were being transmitted accurately to other locations, ancient people believed that the offerings they brought before an idol of a god and the prayers they said in the idol's presence were fully and unfailingly perceived by the god whom that idol represented.[5]

This "was the common way of religion—without exception outside of Israel—in the ancient world. This made it seem entirely normal since no one could find any parallel to the Israelite covenant obligation to worship an invisible God outside of the area of Yahweh's special revelation to his people."[6] Therefore, since idols represented false gods and worshiping one is tantamount to placing a god before the LORD (see #1 above), God consequently forbade the making of idols. Perhaps a modern-day analogy would be if a spouse placed an amorous picture of himself/herself with a previous lover or significant other, who is not their husband/wife, on the wall of the married couple's home—that would be a conflict of interest, drawing one's thoughts and attention to someone other than their spouse. Of course, the spouse is not married to the person in the photograph, but neither is it of propriety for the success of the actual marriage. The second commandment may also be

---

5. Stuart, *Exodus*, 450–451.
6. Stuart, *Exodus*, 451.

stated inversely with the imperative: Worship the LORD your God alone (cf. Deut 6:4)!

3. No Misusing God's Name

The third commandment, or wedding vow, reads, "You shall not make wrongful use of the name of the LORD your God, for the LORD will not acquit anyone who misuses his name" (Exod 20:7 NRSV). This speaks into Israel's relationship with their God in that they are to respect the Name of the LORD and not use it to speak falsely about the One True God. One example from Scripture of taking the LORD's name in vain (NIV) or misusing it (NRSV) comes from an oracle through the prophet Ezekiel to false prophets; in the following passage, every time the word *false* or *falsehood* occurs it is the same Hebrew word (*shawe*) for *wrongful use* or *misuses* (or *vain*) in the third commandment. The LORD God tells Ezekiel,

> Prophesy against the prophets of Israel who are prophesying; say to those who prophesy out of their own imagination: "Hear the word of the LORD!" . . . They have envisioned falsehood and lying divination; they say, "Says the LORD," when the LORD has not sent them, and yet they wait for the fulfillment of their word! Have you not seen a false vision or uttered a lying divination, when you have said, "Says the LORD," even though I did not speak? Therefore thus says the Lord GOD: Because you have uttered falsehood and envisioned lies, I am against you, says the Lord GOD. My hand will be against the prophets who see false visions and utter lying divinations; they shall not be in the council of my people, nor be enrolled in the register of the house of Israel, nor shall they enter the land of Israel; and you shall know that I am the Lord GOD. (Ezek 13:2, 6–9 NRSV)

While it might be thought that only pagans or unbelievers would be the ones who misuses or wrongfully uses God's name, the above passage illuminates how covenant people and even prophets of God speak lies in the name of the LORD; mishandling the authority of God is a severe case of misusing God's personal name.[7] The third "commandment is worded generally enough to encompass any misuse of Yahweh's name—from making light of it or overtly mocking it, to speaking about Yahweh in any way disrespectfully."[8] In a marriage relationship today, perhaps this is equivalent to referring to one's spouse as a ball-and-chain, controlling, manipulative, clueless, etc., to one's friends. The opposite inference, or positive injunction, of this prohibition is: Speak truthfully and respectfully of the Name (and authority) of the LORD God (cf. Matt 6:9b)!

To summarize the first three of the Ten Commandments, or wedding vows, the overarching prohibition is, in a word, idolatry.[9] Idolatry is when one worships, reveres, or even prioritizes anything or anyone above the LORD God. God desires a faithful, monogamous relationship with God's chosen, covenant people, because God has saved, delivered, and liberated his bride and is worthy of his bride's unadulterated worship and devotion.

2.4 Covenant Faithfulness as Obedience to the Law of the LORD

In and throughout wedding ceremonies today, there is copious pontification concerning love. While love is certainly an important element to be celebrated and a legitimate foundation upon which a marriage is established, it is not the only one; equally as significant are trust, respect, honor, commitment, faithfulness, God, and so on, for the couple's life together as marital spouses.

"Love," in the cultural context of the Old Testament, Jon D. Levenson elucidates, "is not an emotion, not a feeling, but a cover term for acts of obedient service.... In the context of covenant, the

---

7. Stuart, *Exodus*, 456.
8. Stuart, *Exodus*, 455–56. Remember: God's personal name is *YHWH* (often translated *LORD*).
9. Janzen, "First Commandments of the Decalogue," 14–24.

alternative to love is not neutrality but rebellion."[10] Appropriately, then, to love God is to keep God's commandments (Exod 20:6; Deut 7:9; Dan 9:4; cf. John 14:15; 1 John 5:3)![11]

Naturally, when a couple stands at the altar (actual or functional) making vows to one another, they have the truest intentions in keeping those verbal commitments. One or the other (or both) are not saying "till death do us part" and simultaneously thinking, "I hope s/he dies early so I can remarry"; likewise, they are not pledging their faithfulness to one another while mentally scheming an extramarital affair in the same moment—far from it! Marriage vows are what the spouses *want* to do.

The same is also true of collective Israel when she makes vows with God in entering covenant relationship: they truly intend to keep their commitments, to obey the commandments of the LORD God[12]—they are eager to do so, for the LORD God had radically rescued and liberated them (cf. Exod 20:2)! The Israelites' enthusiasm of fulfilling the Mosaic/Sinaitic Covenant as *get-to*s instead of *have-to*s is especially perceptible in the context of Israel's recent enslavement and exodus. Juxtaposing what might seem like authoritarian and rigid commandments with the previous centuries of slavery denotes the goodness of the law of the LORD and the desire to uphold it, even as modern marriage vows are *get-to*s not *have-to*s. Indeed, in Rabbinic thought a prohibition (*don't*) is certainly that, yet it also conveys and enjoins the opposite (positive) inference (*do*).[13] Accordingly, if we think about what the Ten Commandments implicitly imply through opposite inference, we can see how these prohibitions are actually liberating.[14]

---

10. Levenson, *Love of God*, 4, 7–8.

11. Speaking of natural marriage between husband and wife, Hamilton ("Marriage [OT and ANE]," *ABD*, 4:568) concludes: "Marriage, then, is essentially a bond of covenant loyalty."

12. The Mosaic/Sinaitic Covenant is comprised of 613 laws, and roughly all (603) of them further detail and develop the broad brushstrokes of the Ten Commandments.

13. One only has the read the Talmud and Midrash to see this interpretive analysis at work in flying colors.

14. Here the methodologies of liberation theology and ideological

Marriage

For example, the first commandment, "you shall have no other gods before me" (Exod 20:3 NRSV), is liberating in its singularity instead of worshiping the myriad of gods in the Egyptian pantheon. Now, whether the Hebrew people worshiped the Egyptian gods is not exactly known (though cf. again Ezek 23). Nevertheless, in contrast to the Egyptians, worshiping one supreme God is far less burdensome than worshiping (or appeasing) a multitude of gods.

To take another example, the fourth commandment is: "Remember the sabbath day, and keep it holy. Six days you shall labor and do all your work. But the seventh day is a sabbath to the LORD your God; you shall not do any work . . ." (Exod 20:8–10 NRSV). After spending four centuries in Egypt enslaved in manual labor 24/7, and being cruelly and ruthlessly oppressed all the while, to having one day off a week is an amazing prospect! This day off, further, is for Israel to remember her salvation (Deut 5:15). While one day off work a week is a relief, it also takes great trust in God that daily needs will still be met even though labor ceases for a day (cf. Exod 16).

Therefore, whether Israel's opportunity is to have a one-day-a-week holiday or to worship one God, or to respect one's neighbor by being generous ("do not steal"), honoring her life ("do not murder"), respecting one other's marital commitment ("do not commit adultery"), or being content ("do not envy"), these are all ways in which God's covenant people may show their love to their covenant partner. These (marital or covenant) vows and commitments are truly *get-to*s instead of *have-to*s. Therefore, the Ten Commandments, along with all the other commands, were not non-consensual, mean-spirited, authoritarian dogma; rather, they are the liberative quality of marital (covenantal) life to express and channel love (worship) of God appropriately.

---

criticism are being touched upon; see, e.g., Gutiérrez, *Theology of Liberation*, and Davies, *Biblical Criticism*, 64–82, respectively.

2.5 Homemaking: Entering and Settling the Promised Land

Typically, after a wedding ceremony and reception, the newly wedded couple departs for a honeymoon; and following the honeymoon, the happy couple settles into their home together, notwithstanding all the preparations made beforehand. While God and the Israelites do not directly depart from their wedding venue of Mt. Sinai (they stayed there one year and construct the tabernacle [Num 9]) and whereas their post-wedding journey cannot be characterized as romantic (grumbling typifies the journey in the wilderness [Num 14–17]), eventually God and the Israelites nestle into their new home. The act of setting up their home in the promised land, after the marriage-like ceremony between God and Israel, is anticipated at Mt. Sinai (Exod 23) and it is revisited at the border of Canaan (Deuteronomy), which then materializes (Joshua-Judges).

In a foregone era, the groom would bring his new bride to their home and pick her up, carrying her over the threshold of the house; this signified they were now making the present house their home together (at least this is in the old movies). In a similar way, God may figuratively be seen as pausing at the threshold of the promised land to review the (marriage) covenant terms with (spouse) Israel (Deut 5) before ushering his bride into the land by dramatically splitting the Jordan River to enter it together (Josh 3). Both at the threshold of the promised land (Deut 7) and at Mt. Sinai (Exod 23:20–33) God tells Israel the way the home (promised land) must be settled in order to protect the sanctity of their marriage relationship. God's intentions are as follows.

> When my angel goes in front of you, and brings you to the Amorites, the Hittites, the Perizzites, the Canaanites, the Hivites, and the Jebusites, and I blot them out, you shall not bow down to their gods, or worship them, or follow their practices, but you shall utterly demolish them and break their pillars in pieces. You shall worship the LORD your God, and I will bless your bread and your water; and I will take sickness away from among you. No

one shall miscarry or be barren in your land; I will fulfill the number of your days.... I will set your borders from the Red Sea to the sea of the Philistines, and from the wilderness to the Euphrates; for I will hand over to you the inhabitants of the land, and you shall drive them out before you. You shall make no covenant with them and their gods. They shall not live in your land, or they will make you sin against me; for if you worship their gods, it will surely be a snare to you. (Exod 23:23-26, 31-33 NRSV)

There are two major themes in this passage. First, the soon-to-be home is the same promised land (the land of Canaan) specified to Abraham (Gen 15) and reiterated to Isaac and to Jacob. Second, the exclusivity of faith, devotion, loyalty, and fidelity which God expects from Israel is made known. The warning to not make a covenant with the inhabitants of the land of Canaan and/or their gods is naturally forbidden, since the Israelites are already in a (marriage) covenant with the LORD their God.[15]

This home that God and the Israelites will make together involves a few preliminary courses of action, since the promised land was already occupied by other peoples. An equivalent analogy would be a groom-to-be who owned a house and leased it to some renters up until the time when he wanted to move into that house with his future wife; the groom-to-be gives his renters ample notice and a date to be moved out of the house because both he and his to-be-bride will be moving into that house after their wedding ceremony to set up their home together. However, the renters do not move out by the specified time and the wedding day has come, so the groom now must physically evict the renters. Consequently, all the renters' belongings are still in the house. Naturally, the bride and groom want all the renters' stuff out of the house for a couple reasons; first, so that there is space in which to move in their own belongings, and, second, the newlyweds do not want anything in their house from the previous renters because they do

---

15. "It should be noted that ... Deut 7:3, forbids intermarriage with the seven peoples to be dispossessed from the land, but does not name other foreigners" (Hamilton, "Marriage [OT and ANE]," *ABD*, 4:564).

not want to be reminded of them. Continuing the analogy, since the groom has physically evicted the renters from his house, he delegates to his bride the job of throwing out all of the furniture, wall hangings, and other belongings of the renters onto the street so that the city garbage trucks can haul it away. Everything must be extracted from the house so that the deleterious connotations are removed from the newlyweds' house.

Now, this is not a likely scenario; but it is nevertheless figuratively equivalent to what transpires in the books of Joshua and Judges. The land which God promised to Abraham centuries earlier, which is God's to gift (cf. Lev 25:23), has been occupied by various people group (Gen 15:18–21). At this point in time, God allows the Israelites to inherit the land and inhabit it (cf. Gen 15:16). God's figurative evicting is the literal militaristic conquest depicted in Josh 6–12; the fighting that God led and the victory that God enabled the Israelites to achieve is the removal of its tenants (Lev 25:23b). The part that Israel is to fulfill in the settlement of the land (cf. Josh 13–22) was to figuratively rid the house of the tenants' possessions; the literal counterpart to this is demolishing altars, breaking down cultic pillars, and otherwise removing anything idolatrous that might be a trigger (i.e., a remembrance of the renters) in worshiping other gods (cf. again Exod 23:24, 33). The peril of those religiously pagan articles is the temptation it would invariably be for the Israelites to commit adultery, viz., idolatry, against the LORD God, Israel's spouse and covenant partner.

This temptation leads us to the sad, next stage of God's love story: unfaithfulness.

Excursus B

Vow (or Covenant) Renewal Ceremony

SOMETIMES IN MARRIAGES, a spousal pair will elect to undergo a vow renewal ceremony. Whether this is precipitated by having survived a difficult season in marriage or occasioned by many decades of marital bliss, the vow renewal ceremony is a chance for the couple to recommit themselves to their relationship. Often the vows in a vow renewal ceremony are the same ones uttered on the couple's wedding day, while at other times the vows are transformed and/or augmented to acknowledge the depth and breadth, the maturity and reality of those original vows. Regardless of the particulars, the ceremony is typically sweet and meaningful as a testament of commitment—even enduring faithfulness—is exhibited.

In the Bible, there is a figurative counterpart to the vow renewal ceremony; it is the covenant renewal ritual. This concept is registered in the foundational document of the life and faith of the Israelite identity: Deuteronomy. Moreover, in the New Testament there is also a vow renewal ceremony of sorts associated with the new covenant salvation-relationship with the Triune God. The Old and New Testaments vow renewal ceremonies of the marriage-like covenant relationship will be presented to highlight the robust longevity of covenantal fidelity on God's part as well as the nature of the people's rededication to their Divine covenant partner.

GOD'S LOVE STORY

1. Vow Renewal Ceremony in the Old Testament

In chapter 2 ("Marriage") it was demonstrated how the Israelites entering covenant with God can be metaphorically viewed as entering marriage relationship. Later, when the Israelites refused to enter the promised land, God punished their rebellion by causing that generation to wander in the wilderness for forty years (Num 14). Once the entire exodus generation died in the desert, the second generation of liberated Israelites were afforded the chance to make the same choice at the same location (Num 33; Deut 1). At the threshold of the promised land, will they trust God to enter and acquire the home promised to Abraham?

1.1 Moses

Before entering the land of Canaan, Moses orates the contents of the law of the LORD—which is essentially the entire book of Deuteronomy—to the new generation of Israelites; and this constitutes the covenant, or vow, renewal ceremony. In fact, within the very fabric of the covenant document is legislation concerning the covenant's generational reiteration and recommitment (Deut 29). Thus, after restating the core legislation (Deut 12–26), along with rehearsing the blessings (rewards) for obedience of the laws and curses (punishments) for disobedience of the laws (Deut 27–28), the covenant becomes effective for another generation.[1] The importance of covenantal loyalty and its prosperous outworking is represented well in the following passage.

> Therefore diligently observe the words of this covenant, in order that you may succeed in everything that you do. You stand assembled today, all of you, before the LORD your God . . . to enter into the covenant of the LORD your God, sworn by an oath, which the LORD your God is making with you today; in order that he may establish you today as his people, and that he may be your God, as he promised you and as he swore to your ancestors,

---

1. Craigie, *Deuteronomy*, 326–29.

Vow (or Covenant) Renewal Ceremony

to Abraham, to Isaac, and to Jacob. I am making this covenant, sworn by an oath, not only with you who stand here with us today before the LORD our God, but also with those who are not here with us today. (Deut 29:9–10, 12–15 NRSV)

Thus, the second generation of liberated Israelites (after the original one that came out of Egypt) do recommit to the LORD God and in faith cross into the promised land to settle therein.

1.2 Joshua

Joshua, Moses' successor, is the next to facilitate a covenant (or vow) renewal ceremony. Joshua's first covenant renewal, i.e., his reciting of the law's blessings and curses, appears to also involve the second generation of liberated Israelites as its recipients. Evidently, Josh 8:30–35 enacts what was spoken in Deut 27,[2] dovetailing the same covenant renewal on both sides of the Jordan River, outside and inside the promised land, respectively.

Joshua, like Moses, arbitrates a(nother) covenant (or vow) renewal ceremony near the time of his death for (presumably) the third generation of liberated Israelites, in Josh 24:1–28.[3] While the law of the LORD is not recorded to have been read, Joshua does summarize their salvation history and the people also recount part of their deliverance journey as well. The public address culminates in the following manner.

> So Joshua made a covenant with the people that day, and made statutes and ordinances for them at Shechem. Joshua wrote these words in the book of the law of God; and he took a large stone, and set it up there under the oak in the sanctuary of the LORD. Joshua said to all the people, "See, this stone shall be a witness against us; for it has heard all the words of the LORD that he spoke to

---

2. Nelson, *Joshua*, 119–20; Chambers, "Confirming Joshua," 147.

3. Dozeman, *Joshua 1–12*, 28; Woudstra, *Joshua*, 340–59. Chambers, "Confirming Joshua," 152.

us; therefore it shall be a witness against you, if you deal falsely with your God." (Josh 24:25–27 NRSV)

So far, the Israelites are faithful to the covenant, at least in terms of renewing the covenant with each subsequent generation. Unfortunately, this is where the consistency stops—for a long time. Joshua does not designate a successor; and the next book of the Bible, Judges, witnesses periodic political leaders whom God appoints. Instead of consistent obedience to the law of the LORD, however, by the end of Judges the religious devolution is such that "all the people did what was right in their own eyes" (Judg 17:6; 21:25 NRSV).

1.3 Josiah

Several centuries later (after the rise of the monarchy [1–2 Samuel] and the schism of the country into two separate kingdoms [1–2 Kings]), the law of the LORD was so neglected that it became lost. In a renovation project of the temple, the book of the law was discovered inside the structure's wall. When the book was verified as the law and read, Josiah, king of Judah, was cut to the heart with grief and remorse because he realized how far the people of God had regressed from God's standards (2 Kgs 22). Josiah reads the law before the people of Judah, thereby renewing the covenant made between God and the Israelites and dedicating themselves to faithfully adhere to its commandments (2 Kgs 23).[4] Thence, Josiah reforms the entire country's religious practices and cultic landscape in accordance to what is stipulated in Deuteronomy (2 Kgs 23).

1.4 Ezra

After Josiah mediated the covenantal (or vow) renewal ceremony, as well as the socioreligious reform of the country, the practice of

---

4. Cf. Nelson, *Joshua*, 119.

Vow (or Covenant) Renewal Ceremony

covenant renewal again dropped off for several generations. The southern kingdom of Judah, like the northern kingdom of Israel before it, fell to an invading foreign empire and became exiled. The Judahites spent seventy years in exile in Babylonia and were eventually liberated by Cyrus king of Persia, the subsequent world dominating empire. Upon the Jews' arrival to Jerusalem, the exilic remnant began rebuilding their towns and reestablishing their religion in its societal expression. It is in this context where an ostensible covenant, or vow, renewal ceremony transpires.[5] In Neh 8–10, Ezra leads the remnant in the reading of the law, observing the weeklong Festival of Booths, confessing sins, and worshiping the LORD; and the leaders of the community signed a recommitment, vowing fidelity to God and the LORD's law.

Synthesis

Now, perhaps the law (Deuteronomy) was read to more generations than is recorded in the Old Testament; regardless, there most certainly were generations of Israelites who were ignorant of the covenant, the marital terms or vows, of the relationship they had with the LORD God. Naturally, it is difficult to follow laws, to fulfil terms, of which one is unaware; this would be like a married couple who suddenly realizes they are oblivious to the purpose of marriage and the nature of their commitment, forgetting entirely the vows they spoke at the altar. Under these circumstances, how should the couple relate with one another? Consequently, it is crucial to be cognizant of—even well-versed in—one's marital vows (the law of the LORD) for optimal relational fruitfulness!

---

5. See Duggan, *Covenant Renewal*.

2. Vow Renewal Ceremony in the New Testament

The vow renewal, or covenant renewal, ceremony even finds a counterpart in the New Testament.[6] It does not have to do with the generational reading of the law of the LORD, per se; rather, because Jesus fulfilled the law, Jesus' disciples follow him—the embodiment of the law (and prophets). Accordingly, the new covenant vow renewal ceremony involves Jesus himself.

Jesus inaugurated the new covenant during the annual Festival of Passover, reinterpreting the bread and wine as his body and blood thereby transforming those elements into the Lord's Supper. The elements of Communion or the Eucharist, that is the bread/body and wine/blood, are effectively the covenantal signs of Jesus' new covenant.[7] Thus, Jesus is the Divine partner and his disciples are the (representative) human partners in the new covenant-making ceremony (Luke 22:20; 1 Cor 11:25; cf. Heb 9:15), whose goal is the forgiveness of sins (Matt 26:28; cf. Heb 9:23–28).

When Jesus exhorts his disciples (past, present, future) to "do this in remembrance of me" (Luke 22:19 NRSV; cf. also 1 Cor 11:24) and when Paul likewise states, "For as often as you eat this bread and drink the cup, you proclaim the Lord's death until he comes" (1 Cor 11:26 NRSV), the ongoing interaction of the covenantal signs (substantiating the covenantal promise) is clearly in view. Consequently, regularly partaking in the eucharistic bread and wine is tantamount to reenacting the new covenant ceremony and is typologically analogous to reiterating the vows of said covenant.[8] Therefore, not only is partaking in Communion a covenant (or vow) renewal ceremony, it is itself, when appropriately engaged (cf. 1 Cor 11:17–22, 27–34), a proclamation of the salvific content (the gospel) of Jesus' covenant.[9] Moreover, the opportunity to

---

6. Cf. Whittle, *Covenant Renewal*.

7. See Waters, *Lord's Supper*. Every covenant in the Old Testament had a covenantal promise and sign; see chapter 1.

8. Baptism, along with Communion, is held as the new covenant sign; however, the Christian does not recurrently get baptized as the Christian does receive Communion regularly.

9. More could be extrapolated on this subject; however, to elaborate further

Vow (or Covenant) Renewal Ceremony

confess salvation-relationship vows to "our great God and Savior, Jesus Christ" (Titus 2:13 NRSV) may be undertaken (in contrast to generationally) monthly, weekly, or even daily (cf. Acts 2:46) in community!

---

here would preempt chapter 6, "(Re)Marriage."

3

Unfaithfulness

3.1 Covenant Unfaithfulness as Spiritual Adultery

IN THIS PHASE OF God's love story, we will examine how and when the ideal of marital fidelity, or covenant faithfulness, is not upheld. In metaphoric terms, covenant unfaithfulness is analogous to spiritual adultery; and since idolatry often precipitates covenant unfaithfulness then those idols or false gods represent illicit, extramarital lovers, as Scripture illustrates. Since God ever upholds the covenant (Deut 7:9), the lack of faithfulness to the covenantal or marital terms (namely the first three of the Ten Commandments which forms Israel's vows [see ch. 2]) is transgressed by the (collective) human covenant partner: Israel.[1]

That covenant disobedience is equivalent to spiritual adultery, having an idolatrous affair, or cheating on God is extremely provocative. The reason the Bible utilizes this metaphorical imagery is ostensibly to convey how scandalous anything less than total covenant faithfulness to God really is; furthermore, such evocative language and imagery was probably meant to shock people out of complacency, to rattle people out of the apathy of their spiritually compromised state.[2] The desired outcome of such colorful and

---

1. Cf. Ortlund, *God's Unfaithful Wife*.
2. Kim, "Yhwh as Jealous Husband," 145.

Unfaithfulness

salacious prophetic oracles is repentance on the part of the Israelites and their renewed covenant loyalty, or marital fidelity to God.

The concept of covenant disobedience as analogous to spiritual adultery is presented at the very beginning of Israel's marriage relationship with God, and unfaithfulness on the part of Israel is a depravity which is basically continually present in the covenant relationship between God and God's chosen people. Accordingly, we will examine the first occurrence of unfaithfulness, the golden calf incident (Exod 32); this god, and others, ensnare the Israelites again during the monarchic period (1 Kgs 11–12). Subsequently, a few prophetic texts will suffice to illustrate the pervasive theme of Israel's unfaithfulness; the life and message of Hosea (Hos 1–4) and an oracle in Ezekiel (Ezek 16) are representative of a large body of Scripture on this point. The ancient Near Eastern fertility cults will shed light on the abovementioned biblical texts to better explain the religious rationale for the idolatrous activity, i.e., the spiritual affairs. God also recurrently pursues Israel and vies for Israel's affections, or covenant loyalty, in order to restore their (covenant) relationship; this is particularly in view in Elijah's contest with Baal (1 Kgs 18) and Josiah's reform (2 Kgs 22–23). Throughout, the tensions and conflict of love and loyalty, unfaithfulness and idolatry in God's love story will be acknowledged.

3.2 The Golden Calf Affair

Tragically, the first instance of unfaithfulness against the LORD God, as perfect covenant partner (husband, as it were), took place essentially simultaneous to the wedding-like ceremony between God and Israel. Almost directly after Israel said their *I-do*s they committed spiritual adultery! The golden calf incident, depicted in Exod 32, is theologically and metaphorically that idolatrous affair.

After the people heard God audibly articulate the Ten Commandments (Exod 20:18–21), which is the essence of the marital covenant, and after thrice stating their vows of intent, Moses thence ascended Mt. Sinai to receive additional legislation and blueprints for their mobile sanctuary, the tabernacle (Exod 21–31). This forty-day time frame (Exod 24:18) culminated with those spoken Ten Commandment written with the finger of God upon tablets of stone (Exod 24:12; 31:18).

Meanwhile, at the foot of the mountain the populace grew impatient; not knowing what may have happened to Moses atop the mountain (apparently presuming his death or desertion), they enact alternate plans (Exod 31:1, 23). Aware of this,

> The LORD said to Moses, "Go down at once! Your people, whom you brought up out of the land of Egypt, have acted perversely; they have been quick to turn aside from the way that I commanded them; they have cast for themselves an image of a calf, and have worshiped it and sacrificed to it, and said, 'These are your gods, O Israel, who brought you up out of the land of Egypt!'" (Exod 32:7-8 NRSV)

Having descended, Moses beholds the same scene (Exod 32:19a).

A golden calf, of all things, is scandalous and ironic! In Egypt, one of the plagues the LORD God inflicted was pestilence upon the livestock with the result that the livestock died. This plague was aimed at Hathor, the Egyptian goddess of love and maternity, who was herself represented as a cow! Yet, the LORD God defeated Hathor (see ch. 1). But here the Israelites are worshiping a calf they have made—and worshiping it as the god who brought the Israelites up out of Egypt (Exod 32:4b). How could a defeated god perform such a miracle as liberation and salvation, much less lead the Israelites forth; or, at the very least, how is a juvenile bovine an appropriate pedestal for (the) God(s)?[3]

Moreover, this golden calf affair violates each of the first three of the Ten Commandments—namely, the marital vows between God and Israel.[4] The second commandment is "You shall not

---

3. Some biblical scholars see in the golden calf a connection to Canaanite religion, where Baal was conceived standing upon a calf as a vehicle; see, e.g., Albertz, *Israelite Religion*, 1:144–46.

4. Though the Israelites do not know these commandments are being written by the finger of God on tablets of stone, they did hear God speak these

UNFAITHFULNESS

make for yourself an idol, whether in the form of anything that is in heaven above, or that is on the earth beneath, or that is in the water under the earth" (Exod 20:4 NRSV). Crafting a golden calf is certainly an image and likeness of something on earth (Exod 32:4). Further, the Israelites "offered burnt offerings and brought sacrifices of well-being" to the graven image, then they proceeded "to eat and drink, and rose up to revel" (Exod 32:6 NRSV); this is all characteristic of pagan worship rituals. Consequently, in so worshiping this golden calf the Israelites were violating the first commandment, "You shall have no other gods before me" (Exod 20:3 NRSV). The newly liberated Israelites also violated the third commandment, "You shall not make wrongful use of the name of the LORD your God" (Exod 20:7a NRSV), by reckoning all their actions as "a festival to the LORD" (Exod 32:5 NRSV). Therefore, worshiping anything other than the LORD God is idolatry—it is spiritual unfaithfulness, infidelity, adultery.

To draw a modern analogy, this near instant spiritual faithfulness might be like the following. It is an average wedding ceremony where a man and woman are married, becoming husband and wife. Upon the recessional, they exit the sanctuary and position themselves in the foyer of the church building to greet everyone in the receiving line, accepting congratulates. Just when it's time for everyone to transition to the wedding reception venue suddenly the groom cannot find his bride. She was just here; he turned his back for a moment and now she's gone. Where is she? The groom starts to look around; he checks a dressing room—only to find his brand-new bride having sexual intercourse with one of the groomsmen![5]

That would be unthinkable, reprehensible, absolutely devastating, and horrifically scandalous! It is difficult to image such a scenario taking place on their wedding day—of all days! Yet, this is not an exaggeration of how God viewed the sin of idolatry with the golden calf and the quick order in which Israel fell into that affair.

---

same words nonetheless (Exod 20:1, 19).

5. That the woman is the guilty party in this analogy is only to stay in the vein of God as husband and Israel as wife.

Spiritual adultery or unfaithfulness is like having illicit relations in the context of marriage. That perspective is God's interpretation of what happened with the golden calf incident, viewing covenant as marriage.

3.3 A Second Ceremony

When Moses descended Mt. Sinai to witness the spiritual affair transpiring, he, in his anger, threw down the stone tablets on which were written the Ten Commandments (Exod 32:19b). Viewing this familiar scene through the metaphorical love story lens, the significance of the broken tablets is poignant. If the Ten Commandments are the essence of the marriage covenant (see again ch. 2) and by extension the tablets are like the marriage certificate, then breaking the two tablets is like the ripping up of a freshly signed marriage certificate. Thus, the marriage terms and the marriage itself is effectively nullified.

Subsequently, the narrative relates how two new tables were crafted which again had inscribed upon them the Ten Commandments (Exod 34:1–4). This act is tantamount to going through the marriage ceremony a second time, since there was an idolatrous baulk the first time through. In conjunction with receiving a new marriage certificate, the marriage commitments or terms are also reiterated. In the following passage, God evokes the first three of the Ten Commandments when renewing covenant terms, or marital vows.

> Take care not to make a covenant with the inhabitants of the land to which you are going, or it will become a snare among you. You shall tear down their altars, break their pillars, and cut down their sacred poles (for you shall worship no other god, because the LORD, whose name is Jealous, is a jealous God). You shall not make a covenant with the inhabitants of the land, for when they prostitute themselves to their gods and sacrifice to their gods, someone among them will invite you, and you will eat of the sacrifice. And you will take wives from among

Unfaithfulness

their daughters for your sons, and their daughters who prostitute themselves to their gods will make your sons also prostitute themselves to their gods. You shall not make cast idols. (Exod 34:12-17 NRSV)

Again, the marital vows reiterated are: (1) no other gods except the LORD God (Exod 20:3 || 34:14); no idols/images to worship gods (Exod 20:4-5 || 34:17); (3) no misuse of the LORD's name (Exod 20:7) / "the LORD, whose name is Jealous" (Exod 34:14 NRSV).[6]

These commitments of fidelity are in contradistinction with the spiritual unfaithfulness of the golden calf affair, which is more explicitly registered here in Exod 34 (vs. Exod 20) in the elicit terms of prostitution. Variously translated, Heb. *zanah* means "to commit fornication."[7] This meaning has both a natural (with spouse) and religious (before God) bearing; furthermore, these two demonstrations actually converge in the practice of cultic prostitution—that is, illicit sexual relations with shrine prostitutes in a cultic structure or setting as an act of worship (see further below).

3.4 A (Near) Continual Affair

Unfortunately, what took place at the foot of Mt. Sinai was not a onetime affair; in fact, God's covenant partner was regularly unfaithful to God. Though God mandated the Israelites to remove all pagan object of worship from the promised land once they settle therein (Exod 23:23-33; 34:13-16; cf. ch. 2), the Israelites did not obey God in this regard; consequently, these pagan objects of worship remained in their house, so to speak, and were indeed, as foretold, a snare and stumbling block for Israel's spiritually monogamous relationship with the LORD God. In addition, more

---

6. *Jealousy* is typically understood as a negative trait; yet, see Janowiak, *"I the Lord Your God Am a Jealous God."*

7. *HALOT*, 1:275-76; BDB, 275-76. So *prostitution* (NIV), *whore* (ESV), *harlot* (NASB), etc.

gods and idols were imported into the land of Israel, including the resurfacing of the golden calf!

Following the conquest and settlement of the promised land (Joshua) and the period of the judges (Judges), the Israelite monarchy was established (1–2 Samuel). After an inelegant start with Saul and even with David, the monarchy was firmly established and stabilized under Solomon. God had established a covenant with David (2 Sam 7), promising an everlasting Davidic dynasty; and though David planned to build a temple for the LORD, he was only able to finance and resource it for Solomon to construct and complete (1 Chr 22). Nevertheless, though Solomon had great wisdom, established Israel's farthest-reaching boarder, and had a peaceful and prosperous reign, Solomon did not lead Israel in covenant faithfulness.

> King Solomon loved many foreign women. . . . Among his wives were seven hundred princesses and three hundred concubines; and his wives turned away his heart. For when Solomon was old, his wives turned away his heart after other gods; and his heart was not true to the LORD his God, as was the heart of his father David. (1 Kgs 11:1a, 3–4 NRSV)

Indeed, with many foreign wives came many foreign gods; the gods of other nations whom Solomon worshiped included Ashtoreth of Sidon (Phoenicia), Chemosh of Moab, Milcom/Molech of Ammon, etc. (1 Kgs 11:5–8, 33; cf. 2 Kgs 23:13). God's punishment for Solomon's idolatry was the division of the united monarchy (1 Kgs 11:9–13); the ten northern tribes succeeded forming the northern kingdom, retaining the name *Israel*, and the remaining southern tribe of Judah (with the tribe of Simeon landlocked within) constituted the southern kingdom of *Judah* (1 Kgs 11:26–40).

It is with the successionist Jeroboam where the golden calf re-emerges. In attempts to keep the northern kingdom independent from Jerusalem and its temple (those being a centripetal force), Jeroboam built two shrines in Dan and Bethel (the northern- and southernmost cities, respectively) to provide religious sites for the northern kingdom. "So the king . . . made two calves of gold. He said to the people, 'You have gone up to Jerusalem long enough. Here are your gods, O Israel, who brought you up out of the land of Egypt.' He set one in Bethel, and the other he put in Dan" (1 Kgs 12:28–29 NRSV). Jeroboam also appointed priests and designated religious festivals for the Israelites of the northern kingdom to observe (1 Kgs 12:31–33), which were adverse to God's law.

Thus, Solomon did not keep covenant (1 Kgs 11:6, 11), and this eventually led to the two golden calves and their shrines, which "became a sin" before the LORD God (1 Kgs 12:30 NRSV)—all of which is spiritual adultery with other gods. Therefore, just as the consequence for idolatry was the schism of the kingdom, so continued idolatry brought the two kingdoms to an end (see ch. 4).

3.5 Spiritual Adultery in Hosea and Ezekiel

God exposes the covenant unfaithfulness of both the northern and southern kingdoms through prophets who also call for repentance, to return to the LORD. Hosea prophesying to Israel and Ezekiel prophesying to Judah serve as examples of how God continued to pursue both kingdoms and all Israelites unto covenant loyalty. Through the metaphor of spiritual promiscuity and adultery, God adjures God's covenant partner to prioritize the health and wholeness of their relationship.

"When the LORD first spoke through Hosea, the LORD said to Hosea, 'Go, take for yourself a wife of whoredom and have children of whoredom, for the land commits great whoredom by forsaking the LORD.' So he went and took Gomer daughter of Diblaim" (Hos 1:2–3 NRSV). Based on the multivalent definition of Heb. *zanah* (the key term here and in Exod 34), there are two ways to interpret this: literal/natural or figurative/spiritual. Is Gomer a hooker on the street corner; or, is Gomer, like any other religiously unfaithful person in Israel at the time, spiritually polyamorous? At times throughout the book of Hosea it seems like either definition is evident, and then sometimes it even seems like a convergence could be intended.[8]

Gomer does seem to be maritally unfaithful to Hosea; for, after marriage and bearing three children she leaves him and shacks up with another man. At this juncture, "the LORD said to [Hosea], 'Go, show your love to your wife again, though she is loved by another man and is an adulteress. Love her as the LORD loves the Israelites, though they turn to other gods'" (Hos 3:1 NIV). To do so Hosea must redeem her; and Hosea apparently pays a(nother?) bride-price (cf. "Excursus A"), comprising money and other resources, to receive Gomer again as his wife from her recent lover (Hos 3:2-4).

Gomer, on the other hand, seems to be illustrative of idolatrous Israel. In the following prophetic oracle, which is representative in Hosea, God speaks as a husband to his wayward wife.

> For their mother has played the whore; she who conceived them has acted shamefully. For she said, "I will go after my lovers; they give me my bread and my water, my wool and my flax, my oil and my drink." Therefore I will hedge up her way with thorns; and I will build a wall against her, so that she cannot find her paths. She shall pursue her lovers, but not overtake them; and she shall seek them, but shall not find them. Then she shall say, "I will go and return to my first husband, for it was better with me then than now." She did not know that it was I who gave her the grain, the wine, and the oil, and who lavished upon her silver and gold that they used for Baal. (Hos 2:5-8 NRSV)

The spouse of God is a generational one (which makes the metaphor break down a bit or at least makes it more complex), meaning that while there is reference to a mother and children (Hos 2:5) Israel is really one increasingly depraved spouse. Israel's worship of the Canaanite god Baal is analogized by God as chasing after lovers, and the gifts that she, Israel, gives to her lovers are the sacrifices due the LORD God! God blocking Israel's (figurative)

---

8. Cf. Mays, *Hosea*, 25-26.

path to Baal should be properly seen as a protective measure in efforts to maintain marital fidelity, not as a controlling, domineering gesture.

Paradoxically, the literal and figurative meaning of Heb. *zanah*, in Hosea, synthesizes into one complex expression. Cultic prostitution is the convergence of physical adultery (sex) and spiritual unfaithfulness (idolatry). The following text plainly speaks to this hybridity.

> My people consult a piece of wood, and their divining rod gives them oracles. For a spirit of whoredom has led them astray, and they have played the whore, forsaking their God. They sacrifice on the tops of the mountains, and make offerings upon the hills, under oak, poplar, and terebinth, because their shade is good. Therefore your daughters play the whore, and your daughters-in-law commit adultery. I will not punish your daughters when they play the whore, nor your daughters-in-law when they commit adultery; for the men themselves go aside with whores, and sacrifice with temple prostitutes; thus a people without understanding comes to ruin. (Hos 4:12–14 NRSV)

Isaiah also acutely criticizes the absurdity of worshiping idols as though they were gods; he retorts that from the same felled tree half of it is used to make an idol while the other half is used as firewood for cooking and warming oneself (Isa 44:9–19)! Similarly, the references to a piece of wood and divining rods, in Hos 4, are self-made instruments of idolatry; also, the locations of hilltops and under the shade of trees were cultic hotspots, where, like Wi-Fi, the signal between humans and the gods was (thought to be) the strongest. This spiritual adultery (idolatry) is paired with physical adultery (prostitution); the use and function of temple prostitutes were for one to physically expression a spiritual devotion.

God's judgment of covenant unfaithfulness against God's covenant partner is also spoken through Ezekiel. Like in Hosea, the spiritual adultery analogy is appropriated; and, though it may not seem possible, Ezekiel's prophetic message is even more graphic in nature. The following is a small excerpt from a very extensive and disturbing biblical chapter.

> [You have] prostituted your beauty, offering yourself to every passer-by, and multiplying your whoring. . . . How sick is your heart, says the Lord GOD, that you did all these things, the deeds of a brazen whore; . . . Yet you were not like a whore, because you scorned payment. Adulterous wife, who receives strangers instead of her husband! Gifts are given to all whores; but you gave your gifts to all your lovers, bribing them to come to you from all around for your whorings. So you were different from other women in your whorings: no one solicited you to play the whore; and you gave payment, while no payment was given to you; you were different. Therefore, O whore, hear the word of the LORD. (Ezek 16:25b, 30, 31b–35 NRSV)

A few elements are underscored in this passage. First, the marital relationship clear: God is husband, and Israel is the wife (Ezek 16:32). Second, God accuses Israel of being unfaithful in the covenant relationship. Third, the lovers represent idolatrous, polytheistic worship.[9]

To further understand the religious rationale for such behavior, especially the tandem sexual and spiritual promiscuity, it is helpful to investigate the background of fertility cults in the ancient Near East and its influence on the chosen people of God as portrayed in the Bible.

3.6 Fertility Cults

The ancient Near East attests many fertility cults: religions centered on the procreation of crops and flocks, chiefly.[10] "In the Sumerian and early Old Babylonian religion (2100–1800 B.C.E.)" it was conceptualized that the heavens and the earth were entities who

---

9. For an excellent, well-balance treatment of this passage, see Kim, "Yhwh as Jealous Husband," 127–47.

10. Cf. Klein, "Sacral Marriage," *ABD*, 5:866–70.

were sexually involved with one another.[11] One Sumerian poem substantiates and illustrates the theological outlook of the heavens inseminating the earth for the latter's flourishing; an excerpt reads:

> The holy Earth, the pure Earth, beautified herself
> for holy Heaven,
> Heaven, the noble god, inserted
> his sex into the wide earth,
> Let flow the semen of the heroes, Trees and Reed,
> into her womb.
> The Earthly Orb, the trusty cow,
> was impregnated with the good semen of Heaven.[12]

In the perspective of the fertility cult, then, rain was conceived as the semen of the sky god which showered down on/in the earth which was conceptualized as the earth goddess's womb. The result of this fertilization would be the agricultural sprouting and growth from the land; this fertility yields foodstuff for humans to eat and live and crops for flocks—all vital for agrarian societies.

Canaanite religion also contained aspects of the fertility cults, with the sky god being Baal and Asherah, the goddess of the earth, being his consort. Baal, also held as a warrior god, is mentioned quite often in the Old Testament. Asherah is also present in the Old Testament, though much less frequently; sometimes the reference indicates a goddess, while other occurrences refer to a sacred pole for her veneration.[13] Altars to Baal and sacred poles to Asherah were often situated next to each other (Judg 6:25–30; 2 Kgs 17:16; 21:3–4); although, even a(n Asherah) tree next to an altar of the LORD was expressly prohibited (Deut 16:21), for it would surely lead the Israelites to the worship of other gods.

Furthermore, the issue of shrine or temple prostitutes in Hos 4:12–14 (also 2 Kgs 23:7), in addition to the Asherah poles intimated there,[14] is yet another component of Baal and Asherah

---

11. Weinfeld, "Imagery of God," 525.

12. As quoted in Weinfeld, "Imagery of God," 524. Cf. also Hos 2:21–22.

13. Some scholars believe the Asherah pole was primarily a phallic symbol; cf. Day, "Asherah in the Hebrew Bible," 398; Dever, *Did God Have a Wife?*, 163.

14. Drinkard, "Religious Practices," 209.

worship within the confines of the fertility cult as the intersection of physical and spiritual covenant, or marital, unfaithfulness. Douglas Stuart explains:

> Temple prostitution is described at various points in the Old Testament. Behind it lay the notion that all creation was in fact procreated, so everything that would exist had to be born into existence. When this was coupled with the "sympathetic magic" idea that things done symbolically in one location might cause certain behavior in another, ritual worship sex performed in order to stimulate the gods to produce fertility on earth was the result. Ancient pagan worshipers were taught that if they, taking the symbolic role of, say, Baal, would have sex with a temple prostitute symbolically portraying, say, Asherah, this act would stimulate things to be born on earth: the young of flocks and herds, as well as the seedlings of all desired plants. Sex thus became a regular aspect of idol worship and was . . . widely practiced.[15]

"Therefore," as Douglas Stuart concludes, "when one sacrificed to Baal and engaged in ritual worship sex for Baal, the fertility cult tenets guaranteed that Baal would send rain—it was held to be a direct cause-effect correlation."[16]

However, what would happened if there was a drought throughout the land when, all the while, the fertility cult adherents were *worshiping*? Well, they might *worship* more fervently and frequently. But what if no rain persisted still? How did worshipers of Baal and Asherah reconcile the seemingly failed cause-effect correlation between pagan worship and rain? This exact dilemma reaches a crisis point during the days of the prophet Elijah.

3.7 God Vies for Israel's Affection

God does not passively watch Israel wander into idolatry and idly accept the fate of whatever polytheistic endeavor God's covenant

---

15. Stuart, *Exodus*, 453.
16. Stuart, *Exodus*, 451.

partner gets involved in. Rather, whenever Israel is lured away by other gods, the LORD God pursues his bride. God vying for the affection of Israel is perhaps best seen in the confrontation of Baal (and Asherah) atop Mt. Carmel and the spectacular contest to determine who the true God is.

3.7.1 Elijah

King Ahab of Israel had married the Phoenician princess Jezebel, who brought her worship of Baal (and Asherah) with her to Israel. Ahab adopted the worship of Baal (and Asherah) and thereby largely influenced the religious landscape of the northern kingdom of Israel (see 1 Kgs 16:31–33), just as Solomon did during the united monarchy. Considering the fertility cult aspect of the religion surrounding Baal and Asherah (3.6), God directly confronts its theological tenants and the gods themselves.

God sent Elijah to King Ahab to declare, "As the LORD the God of Israel lives, before whom I stand, there shall be neither dew nor rain these years, except by my word" (1 Kgs 17:1 NRSV). Ostensibly, Ahab understands that this is a confrontation of his sky god (Baal); also, for the Israelite audience well-versed in the law, they are supposed to deduce that a drought is a covenantal punishment for covenantal disobedience or unfaithfulness (cf. Deut 28:22–24).

This drought, and pursuant famine, lasts for three years (1 Kgs 18:1–2; cf. Luke 4:25; Jas 5:17). Subsequently, Elijah relays God's message to Ahab: "I will send rain on the earth" (1 Kgs 18:1 NRSV). Elijah also reiterates the reason for the drought and proposes a resolution to the matter, when accosting Ahab:

> "You have forsaken the commandments of the LORD and followed the Baals. Now therefore have all Israel assemble for me at Mount Carmel, with the four hundred fifty prophets of Baal and the four hundred prophets of Asherah, who eat at Jezebel's table." So Ahab sent to all the Israelites, and assembled the prophets at Mount Carmel. (1 Kgs 18:18b–20 NRSV)

The LORD God plans to challenge Baal and Asherah to again demonstrate that the LORD is God of gods, that there is no other god than the LORD, that God alone is to be worshiped, that no idol is to come between God and the Israelites, that God's name is not to be treated falsely.

The event atop Mt. Carmel is to be viewed as a showdown between the gods. The terms of the contest are that once sacrifices are prepared upon altars, "'you call on the name of your god and I will call on the name of the LORD; the god who answers by fire is indeed God.' All the people answered, 'Well spoken!' (1 Kgs 18:24 NRSV). The agreed-upon terms of the contest are provocative; Baal and the LORD are both considered sky gods,[17] so the god who answers by hurling fire down *from the sky* will be hailed the true God. Let the contest begin!

The prophets of Baal and Asherah beckoned and pleaded with their gods all morning long and into midday to send down fire down from heaven; they danced, performed blood-letting rituals,[18] prophesied frantically, but there was no fire (1 Kgs 18:26-29). After some taunting, next Elijah took his turn. Once an altar was built and a sacrifice prepared—and doused with water (for dramatic effect?)—Elijah prayed in the hearing of all present, and he received the answer to his prayer.

> "O LORD, God of Abraham, Isaac, and Israel, let it be known this day that you are God in Israel, that I am your servant, and that I have done all these things at your bidding. Answer me, O LORD, answer me, so that this people may know that you, O LORD, are God, and that you have turned their hearts back." Then the fire of the LORD fell and consumed the burnt offering, the wood, the stones, and the dust, and even licked up the water that was in the trench. When all the people saw it, they fell on their faces and said, "The LORD indeed is God; the LORD indeed is God." (1 Kgs 18:36-39 NRSV)

17. Cf. Fensham, "Yahweh and Baal in 1 Kings 17–19," 227–36.
18. Drinkard ("Religious Practices," 208) notes: "Such lacerations are usually explained as ecstatic acts or mimetic magic to persuade or cause the deity to release the fructifying rain."

Furthermore, God subsequently sends rains from heaven (1 Kgs 18:41–46), ending the drought and again upstaging Baal. Preeminently, the Israelites profess the LORD is God! In the demonstration on Mt. Carmel, God, in a sense, woos again his bride, his covenant people Israel, winning them over to love and faithfulness to her great God and covenant partner. The religious reformation experienced in the days of Elijah does not, in the end, last long. Nevertheless, there are other times when Baal and Asherah are confronted and the people return to the LORD again.

3.7.2 Josiah

A near equivalent of Elijah's confrontation of Baal and Asherah in the northern kingdom (Israel) is experienced later in the southern kingdom (Judah) under the reign of King Josiah. Josiah's predecessors, especially Manasseh (2 Kgs 21:1–9), had erected altars to Baal and poles to Asherah, thereby seducing the nation to worship gods other than the LORD God. However, in his socioreligious reform (see "Excursus B"), Josiah destroyed all of Baal's altars and tore down all Asherah poles (2 Kgs 23:1–20; cf. also 2 Kgs 11:18; 18:22).

Unlike Elijah who received a divine directive to confront Baal, Josiah's reform was catalyzed in finding lost book of the law of the LORD (see 2 Kgs 22). It was in the covenant, the founding document of Israelite culture and religion, that God's will—which previously had faded from memory—became known, namely in terms of worshiping the LORD God alone and not crafting images of other gods. Naturally, it was in the marriage certificate or vows, i.e., the book of the law/covenant (2 Kgs 22:8, 11 / 2 Kgs 23:2, 21) or Deuteronomy, that Judah understood what her intended relationship with God was and how to fulfill it.

3.7.3 Hosea

Time and time again, God pursues and woos wayward Israel to beckon her to return to God, to love God, to express covenantal loyalty and devotion to God. To cite Hosea again, God is seen actively trying to salvage their relationship; God expresses:

> Therefore, I will now allure her, and bring her into the wilderness, and speak tenderly to her. . . . On that day, says the LORD, you will call me, "My husband," and no longer will you call me, "My Baal." For I will remove the names of the Baals from her mouth, and they shall be mentioned by name no more. (Hos 2:14, 16–17 NRSV)

These conciliatory measures are incredibly enduring. The wilderness reference is citing the forty years of wandering in the wilderness (see Num 14). Even though the wilderness wanderings was a time of testing from God and rebellion of the Israelites, God nevertheless recounts the silver-lining of those forty years—namely, how during that time Israel learned how she was dependent upon the LORD God for food, water, protection from hostile nomads, etc. Additionally, Israel did not have nearly as many distractions in the desert regarding worshiping other gods of other peoples; it was just them and God. So, God wants to allure his bride back to the desert to restore their relationship and strengthen their relationship for the future—just like a marriage retreat is designed with the goals of relational restoration and strengthening for reengagement of life together!

How will God's love story continue to develop? We must keep reading through the Old Testament to find out.

Excursus C

Risk of Relationship

THE FACT THAT A perfect God would initiate intimate relationship with an imperfect people, as in the case of the Israelites with the Mosaic/Sinaitic Covenant, is definitely a calculated risk. The high probability for unfaithfulness in that relationship on the part of the fallen human representative makes God extremely vulnerable (see ch. 4). It is a wonder that God elects to engage humanity intimately in relationship; yet this is God's design from the very beginning (Gen 1–2) and right through to the end (Rev 21–22).

1. Adam & Eve: Genesis 1–3

Even before sin entered the world, it was still a calculated risk for God to be in relationship with humankind. The original humans had a choice; they could eat from the Tree of Life or the Tree of the Knowledge of Good and Evil. However, instead of obeying God, trusting they were already like God as image bearers (Gen 1:27; 3:4–5), and fulfilling their role in governing creation as God's vice-regents (Gen 1:28; 3:1, 13), Adam and Eve violated God's one prohibition, rebelled against the Creator, and introduced sin and death into the world (cf. Gen 2:16–17). Bruce Birch poignantly remarks, "God takes the risk of a relationship that allows genuine freedom and is willing to be the first victim of a broken relationship when the man and the woman choose disobedience (Genesis 3)."[1]

Forever after, humans are afforded the choice of good, of right relationship. In the law, the two options of obedience and disobedience, good and evil are put before Israel (e.g., Deut 1:39); in Judges, "all the people did what was right in their own eyes" (Judg 17:6b; 21:25b NRSV), which was actually quite wicked; in Proverbs, wisdom and folly are figurative paths in which the wise and fool walk respectively—and the Tree of Life is even a symbol there of that which is good and right (Prov 3:18; 11:30; 13:12; 15:4). Invariably, humans' propensity for sin recurrently ruptures meaningful and satisfying relationship with both God and others.

2. Jesus in the New Testament

In Jesus, does God risk any less in relationship when inaugurating the new covenant? No; in fact, God is risking even more, when entering an eternal grace-based covenant with humanity. Though salvation—the crux of the new covenant—is free for the (collective) human covenant partner upon God's grace through faith in Christ (Eph 2:7–9), in order to establish the new covenant Jesus had to pay the ultimate price—his own perfect life as a sacrifice (Mark 10:45; Eph 1:7; 1 Cor 7:23; Gal 3:13–15; Titus 2:14; 1 Pet 2:24; 1 John 2:2). For God, therefore, the relational risk is excessively great.

The grace which God grants in Jesus, then, is extremely costly and precious; yet, the human new covenant partner may interact with it as though it were cheap grace.[2] In these instances, the erring Christian exploits grace to justify sinning (cf. Rom 3:5–8; 6:1–2, 15;) or even using God's grace as a license to sin (cf. 1 Pet 2:16; Jude 4); the implications are damnable, according to Scripture (Heb 6:4–6; 10:26–27; 2 Pet 2:20–21). Instead, the persons

---

1. Birch, "Moral Trajectory of the Old Testament," 7.
2. Bonhoeffer, *Cost of Discipleship*, 45–60.

saved by grace through faith has their sins acquitted them which makes right relationship possible because of Jesus' great achievement on the cross (redemption), producing an ever humble and grateful life-posture before the Savior. Thus, there is relational risk for the human new covenant partner as well.

Relationship (marital or otherwise) is optimal when both parties are equally and wholly invested in it; this is acutely the case in the new covenant. Jesus gave up his life for those whom he saves; similarly, those who receive and experience salvation do so by giving up their life to Jesus. Indeed, Jesus said, "If any want to become my followers, let them deny themselves and take up their cross daily and follow me" (Luke 9:23 NRSV), meaning the Christian continually dies to the old (unregenerate) self and recurrently shares in the risen life and cause of Christ as is the lifestyle befitting new creatures in Christ (2 Cor 5:17). Thus, the salvation reality is as Paul has said: "It is no longer I who live, but it is Christ who lives in me" (Gal 2:20 NRSV).

It is by the Holy Spirit, or the spirit of Jesus/Christ (Acts 16:7; Phil 1:19 / Rom 8:9; 1 Pet 1:11), that enables this new life, beginning at the transformative regeneration of an individual (John 3:3–5; Titus 3:4–7; cf. 1 Pet 1:2–3). The same Spirit of the Living God indwells and resides within Jesus' disciples (John 20:22; Rom 8:9–11; 1 Cor 3:16; 6:19) for the mystical union of salvation-relationship (cf. John 14:23; 15:1–17). As a result, the Holy Spirit—who sanctifies the saint (Rom 15:16; 1 Cor 6:11; 1 Thess 4:7–8; 2 Thess 2:13)—is God's deposit of God's own self (with)in the disciple of Christ, in order that the human is able and empowered to keep covenant faithfulness (cf. John 13:34). Therefore, while the risk of new covenant relationship between Jesus and the bride of Christ is still great, the (envisioned, intended) investment and outcome is greater still!

4

Divorce

4.1 Divorce, the Problematic Concept

AS THOUGH APPROXIMATELY A millennium of covenant unfaithfulness (or spiritual adultery) on the part of the Israelites is not bad enough,[1] the covenant relationship between God and the Israelites deteriorates still further. The next stage of God's love story is, in metaphorical terminology, divorce; in literal terms it is exile. This is how the prophets speak of the nadir of the Israelites' covenantal experience and its repercussions.

Before grappling with these difficult texts and this disturbing topic, a few disclaimers must be made. On the face of it, divorce is the opposite of God's intention for a marriage relationship (Deut 22:19, 29; Mal 2:16); so, why is it that God initiates a—yes, even metaphoric—divorce? While divorce was far from ideal for husband and wife, it was permitted on exception in the law (Deut

---

1. That the total unfaithfulness period is roughly 1,000 years takes into consideration the first act of idolatry (Exod 32) within the parameters of the Mosaic/Sinaitic Covenant and continuing almost uninterruptedly until the time that Israel (722 BCE) and then Judah (586 BCE) are exiled (2 Kgs 17, 24–25). First Kings 6:1 annotates Solomon's temple construction began 480 years after the exodus (cf. 1 Kgs 6:38); and after Solomon's death (cf. 1 Kgs 11:42) the united monarchy splits (in 930 BCE). Thus, adding together all the evidence from Scripture yields this time frame to be about 860 years.

24:1-4; cf. Matt 5:31-32; Matt 19:1-12 // Mark 10:1-12; see also 1 Cor 7:10-13). Jesus, addressing the abuses of divorce proceedings in his day, namely the wide latitude taken to absolve marriages,[2] teaches, "It was because you were so hard-hearted that Moses allowed you to divorce your wives, but from the beginning it was not so. And I say to you, whoever divorces his wife, except for unchastity, and marries another commits adultery" (Matt 19:7-9 NRSV).

According to Jesus, therefore, the only grounds for divorce is marital unfaithfulness.[3] Jesus speaks here of physical unfaithfulness (cf. also Matt 5:27-30); could the same be true of spiritual adultery, that is, an idolatrous affair with another god? Indeed, spiritual adultery is ostensibly God's justification for a metaphorical divorce in the Old Testament; or, in literal terms, Israel's perpetual egregious covenant disobedience is met with exile. While the subject is still problematic, perhaps with this insight the character of God is palatable.

What lies before us to investigate in this phase of divorce, then, is the following. First, the paradox of God's faithfulness in the face of the Israelites' unfaithfulness and God's ensuing annulment of the marriage, or covenant, is explored. Second, the metaphorical (divorce) and literal (breaking/broken covenant) expressions of said annulment in Scripture are examined. Third, the natural (exile) and figurative (thrown out of the house) implications of the metaphorical divorce between God and the Israelites is elucidated. Fourth, the promises and hopes for relational reconciliation will be inspected; the return from exile to the promised land and prophecy of a new covenant are the basis for this restoration. Finally, the tensions and ambiguities in the latest writings of the Old Testament as to whether reconciliation and right relationship is actualizing is registered and the question suspended.

---

2. See Collins, "Marriage (NT)," *ABD*, 4:570; cf. also Wall, "Divorce," *ABD*, 2:217-19.

3. For Paul's case of desertion, see 1 Cor 7:10-11. I am also aware of the concern for regarding whether physical abuse qualifies as a legitimate reason for divorce; see, e.g., Roberts, *Not under Bondage*.

4.2 Marital Tensions: The Unfaithfulness of the Israelites and the Faithfulness of God

In the tragic pattern of Israel's idolatry which lasted for several centuries, God dramatically intervened several times in order to salvage relationship with Israel, God's covenant people, in the hopes that they might reform their idolatrous disposition to a state of complete devotion, love, and worship of the LORD God alone (see ch. 3). Despite these interventions, however, Israel did not repent and reform in perpetuity, but only periodically. God's covenant partner appears to be (at times) indifferent to God; the Israelites would rather play the harlot than be loyal to the LORD to be blessed by God, generally speaking.

The time eventually came when God no longer extended mercy; rather, God executed punishment upon the Israelites by causing them to experience the consequences of their sin of marital unfaithfulness. Consequently, after nearly a millennium of marital unfaithfulness the LORD God divorced his wife. Still, even if it is granted that God was faithful to his spouse in the face of Israel's unfaithfulness, isn't bringing that marriage to an end also the expiration of faithfulness? How can this apparent contradiction, or paradox, be resolved?

The faithfulness of God is a well-known attribute of God, the substance of doctrine and theology; yet, consider this concept again in the context of marital (covenant) relationship. "Know therefore that the LORD your God is God, the faithful God who maintains covenant loyalty with those who love him and keep his commandments, to a thousand generations" (Deut 7:9 NRSV; cf. Deut 32:4); "The LORD is faithful in all his words, and gracious in all his deeds" (Ps 145:13b NRSV). Scriptural statements of God's faithfulness are often situated among other characteristics of God which help to nuance the extent or nature of God's faithfulness.

On this point, God's self-identification to Moses atop Mt. Sinai is remarkable: "The LORD, the LORD, a God merciful and gracious, slow to anger, and abounding in steadfast love and faithfulness, keeping steadfast love for the thousandth generation,

Divorce

forgiving iniquity and transgression and sin, yet by no means clearing the guilty, but visiting the iniquity of the parents upon the children and the children's children, to the third and the fourth generation" (Exod 34:6-7 NRSV). These attributes of the LORD God are the most consistent and pervasive description and witness throughout the Old Testament (see Num 14:18; 2 Chr 30:9; Neh 9:17, 31; Pss 86:15; 103:8; 111:4; 145:8; Joel 2:13; Jonah 4:2).[4] Significantly, the initial revelation of God's character and attributes is set within the context of the golden calf affair (cf. chs. 3 and 4); consequently, God's grace, mercy, abounding love and faithfulness yielding a slow anger is the reality throughout the marriage-like covenant relationship between God and Israel (cf. Exod 34:7). Notwithstanding, divorce is seen as the much-delayed consequence for several centuries of marital unfaithfulness, idolatry: worshiping other gods over against the LORD God, making idols and worshiping them, and treating the name of the LORD contemptuously and without reverence.

To reconcile the paradox, then, of God being faithful (thesis) on the one hand and God metaphorically divorcing his bride on the other (antithesis), is the solution (synthesis) that God is just[5]—even still, God's is a justice (getting *exactly* what one deserves) tempered with grace (getting what one *does not* deserve) and mercy (*not* getting what one *does* deserve), which is itself a paradox![6] Therefore, God's punishment of God's covenant partner, or bride, is not unbridled, irrational wrath; rather, it is just (cf. Deut 30:11-20). Indeed, "it is unthinkable that God would do wrong, that the Almighty would pervert justice" (Job 34:12 NIV); "for the LORD is righteous; he loves righteous deeds; the upright shall behold his face" (Ps 11:7 NRSV).

Consequently, God is completely faithful to his spouse. Despite belligerent and/or unintentional unfaithfulness (covenantal disobedience) on the part of the Israelites, the LORD God is

---

4. Cf. Limburg, *Jonah*, 90.

5. These parenthetical terms are the nomenclature of German philosopher Hegel's *dialectics*, a notion akin to *paradox*.

6. See Keller, *Generous Justice*.

faithful regardless. Nevertheless, in the long-term what may have seemed to be faithlessness is tough love, and the faithfulness of God in this regard is seen in dramatic fashion (see ch. 5).

4.3 Annulling the Marriage

4.3.1 Certificate of Divorce

When the LORD metaphorically divorces the Hebrew people because of marital unfaithfulness God does not do so rashly, hastily, or flippantly. But eventually there came a point when God exacted justice for marital unfaithfulness. "Thus says the Lord GOD: None of my words will be delayed any longer, but the word that I speak will be fulfilled, says the Lord GOD" (Ezek 12:28 NRSV).

Finally, God divorced Israel—nullifying the marriage-like covenant. Through two different prophets, God spoke of the issuing of a divorce certificate. Jeremiah conveys:

> The LORD said to me in the days of King Josiah: Have you seen what she did, that faithless one, Israel, how she went up on every high hill and under every green tree, and played the whore there? And I thought, "After she has done all this she will return to me"; but she did not return, and her false sister Judah saw it. She saw that for all the adulteries of that faithless one, Israel, I had sent her away with a decree of divorce; yet her false sister Judah did not fear, but she too went and played the whore. Because she took her whoredom so lightly, she polluted the land, committing adultery with stone and tree. Yet for all this her false sister Judah did not return to me with her whole heart, but only in pretense, says the LORD. (Jer 3:6–10 NRSV)

In this passage Judah was supposed to take a lesson from what happened to Israel. Israel was issued a certificate of divorce (or, in natural terms, exiled by the Assyrians) for long-standing spiritual adultery (idolatry), and so Judah was supposed to return to God in forsaking idolatry and be loyal to the covenant in order to avert the same fate (see 4.4.1 below). However, Judah did not heed God's warning; instead, Judah returned "only in pretense"—that is, merely going through the motions of repentance and having the veneer of contrition. The consequent grievous judgment of God, therefore, is: "Faithless Israel is more righteous than unfaithful Judah" (Jer 3:11 NIV).

Like Jeremiah, Isaiah relates, "Thus says the LORD: Where is your mother's bill of divorce with which I put her away? Or which of my creditors is it to whom I have sold you? No, because of your sins you were sold, and for your transgressions your mother was put away" (Isa 50:1 NRSV).[7] God's bride, Israel, is sometimes referred to as two sisters (as in Jer 3) because of how the nation divided into two. Isaiah's oracle, which references "your mother's bill of divorce," is addressed to the generation of Judeans in Babylonian exile, hence the mother is the previous generation whom God had exiled. Consequently, exile is the literal counterpart to the metaphorical expression of certificate of divorce; yet, before the exile is more closely examined, attention must be focused on the implications of a broken covenant, which is the effect of a certificate of divorce.

4.3.2 A Broken Covenant

Whereas divorce is a metaphorical articulation in the prophetic material, there is also nonfigurative language articulated in the prophets substantiating the same reality. In literal terms, God speaks of how the Israelites have been *breaking the covenant* with the result that God evaluates it to be a *broken covenant* eventually. Thus, just as the Bible witnesses the making of covenants it also acknowledges the breaking of covenants.

- "The earth lies polluted under its inhabitants; for they have transgressed laws, violated the statutes, broken the everlasting covenant." (Isa 24:5 NRSV; cf. Deut 31:16–22)

---

7. Though the phrasing differs between Jer 3 ("decree of divorce") and Isa 50 ("bill of divorce"), the Heb. terminology is the same in each passage: *sepher kerithuth*, document of divorcement.

- "They have turned back to the iniquities of their ancestors of old, who refused to heed my words; they have gone after other gods to serve them; the house of Israel and the house of Judah have broken the covenant that I made with their ancestors." (Jer 11:10 NRSV; cf. Lev 26:14–15)
- "You have broken my covenant with all your abominations." (Ezek 44:7b NRSV)
- "I took my staff Favor and broke it, annulling the covenant that I had made with all the peoples." (Zech 11:10 NRSV; cf. Hos 8:1)

Furthermore, it is important to distinguish between Israel violating the covenant and breaking the covenant. In the former case, Israel frequently transgresses the covenant commandments while God remains mercifully faithful to the covenant terms; in the latter phenomenon, after nearly a millennium of Israel's covenant unfaithfulness, God justly judges and punishes the Israelites, appraising the covenant to be severely compromised if not irrevocably damaged. Notwithstanding, God is never the covenant partner who violates, i.e., is involved in breaking, the Mosaic/Sinaitic Covenant (Judg 2:1; cf. Lev 26:44).

4.4 Separation and Estrangement

A severed marriage naturally results in separation and relational estrangement. This is seen in the case of God and Israel naturally through the exile and figuratively as Israel being kicked out of the house, or the promised land. These are the fallout measures, the consequences of the broken relationship due to wayward idolatry.

4.4.1 Exile

Exile is a punishment for covenantal unfaithfulness, as stipulated in the law (see Lev 26:33–44; Deut 4:27; 28:36–41, 63–68; 29:28;

30:4; 32:26);[8] and it may be viewed as the ultimate covenantal curse due to it being the most severe corrective and final punitive measure. *Exile* (noun) is the state or a period of forced absence from one's country or home; *the act of being exiled* (verb) is the banishment from one's own country or home. Exile was the fate for both the northern kingdom (Israel) and the southern kingdom (Judah).

It will be remembered that because Solomon married foreign woman resulting in his adopting the worship of the foreign (false) gods of his wives, God tore apart the united monarchy in 930 BCE (cf. ch. 3). From there, the northern kingdom of Israel saw nineteen kings who ruled the country over a period of about two hundred years; essentially every king of Israel was evil (cf. 2 Kgs 10:30–31). The southern kingdom of Judah had eight out of twenty monarchs who were righteous over an approximate 325-year span. In every case where the evaluative statement of a monarch is either "did what was right in the sight of the LORD" or "did what was evil in the sight of the LORD" in 1–2 Kings,[9] the standard of that judgment is based on the Mosaic/Sinaitic Covenant; more specifically, the evil referred to is all under the umbrella of idolatry—the violation of the first three of the Ten Commandments, namely, which are the same wedding vows between the covenant partners God and all the Israelites.

Whereas God's initial punishment of national idolatry was the schism of the country, the ongoing idolatry of both kingdoms is eventually met with exile, banishing people from the land. Regarding Israel, the Assyrian Empire brought an end to Israel in 722 BCE; the Assyrians' method of exile was assimilation, relocating and scrambling people groups so that consensus and consequently revolt could not occur (2 Kgs 17). Concerning Judah, the Babylonian Empire (the subsequent world power) caused Judah's demise in 586 BCE; after destroying the city of Jerusalem and burning down the temple (2 Kgs 24), the Babylonians deported most of

---

8. Citations compiled by Stuart in *Hosea–Jonah*, xxxvii.
9. These refrains occur approximately thirty times in 1–2 Kgs.

Judah's population, through three deportations (2 Kgs 24 // Jer 52), to Babylon as captives (2 Kgs 25).

The length of the exile, specifically as it relates to the Judeans in Babylonia, was prophesied by Jeremiah. God foretells,

> This whole land shall become a ruin and a waste, and these nations shall serve the king of Babylon seventy years. Then after seventy years are completed, I will punish the king of Babylon and that nation, the land of the Chaldeans, for their iniquity, says the LORD, making the land an everlasting waste. (Jer 25:11–12 NRSV; cf. Jer 29:10; Dan 9:2; 2 Chr 36:20–23; Ezra 1:1–4)

Foreign empires consequently serve as God's punishment tool against God's covenant partner; God orchestrates Assyria to punish Israel (Isa 10:5–7), Babylon to punish Judah (Isa 13:1–5; Jer 50:18), and Persia to punish Babylon, thereby releasing the Judean exiles (cf. Jer 25:8–12).

4.4.2 Thrown Out of the House

At the cusp of the Israelites becoming exiled, i.e., forcibly removed from their homeland and displaced in another location, Scripture sometimes also speaks of this event as how God had "banished/expelled them from his presence" (2 Kgs 17:20 / 2 Kgs 24:20; Jer 52:3) or "removed them/Israel out of his sight" (2 Kgs 17:18; 24:3 / 2 Kgs 17:23).[10] These expressions stand halfway between the natural verbiage of exile and its figurative counterpart whose language evokes the unfaithful partner getting kicked out of the house by the partner who was cheated on. Indeed, while mitigating circumstances vary, it is typically the unfaithful partner who is extracted from the couple's residence. Regardless, in divorce there is innately a holistic separation of the couple.

If God and the Israelites living together in the promised land was metaphorical of marriage, then God removing the Israelites

---

10. These statements apply both to Israel and Judah; 2 Kgs 17 references concern the northern kingdom, and 2 Kgs 24 (and Jer 52) references concern the southern kingdom.

from the promised land is metaphorical of divorce. God had stipulated in the law that when a husband had an adulterous wife, he could divorce her and thrust her out of the house (Deut 24:1). Likewise, God divorced, or thrust his bride(s) out of her (their) homeland.

The issue of a homeland, it will be remembered, was extremely important to the Hebrew people! God's betrothal promises to the patriarchs included land, descendants, and blessings (see ch. 1). In the context of marriage, the Mosaic/Sinaitic Covenant also has these three elements encapsulated in it. Previously we examined the major crux of the covenant, the first three of the Ten Commandments (see ch. 2); yet, when considering its broader context, the Israelites also said *I do* to the stipulations concerning blessings and curses as well—and these include (among other things) the increasing or decreasing of land, descendants, and blessings.

In the Mosaic/Sinaitic Covenant, that marriage-like contract, God stipulated, "If you will only obey the LORD your God, by diligently observing all his commandments . . ." (Deut 28:1 NRSV), then (1) regarding land: God will give a good and fertile land to be enjoyed (Deut 28:8, 12; cf. Lev 26:4–5, 10–11); (2) regarding descendants: God will grant fruitfulness in procreation and flourishing of the nation (Deut 28:4, 9, 11; Lev 26:9); (3) regarding blessings: there will be economic success and agricultural prosperity (Deut 28:3–6; cf. Lev 26:12–13).

"But if you will not obey the LORD your God by diligently observing all his commandments . . ." (Deut 28:15a NRSV), then (1) regarding land: Israel will be besieged, cities destroyed, and the Israelites uprooted from the land (Deut 28:50–52, 63; cf. Lev 26:33–35, 43), i.e., exile; (2) regarding descendants: the Israelite population will be drastically reduced through premature death, starvation, etc. (Deut 28:62–63; cf. Lev 26:22), because of the events leading up to exile; (3) regarding blessings: punishments (curses), or the absence or removal of blessings, are administered by God (Deut 28:16–19; Lev 26:18, 21, 23–24, 27–28).

Therefore, the ultimate covenantal punishment was exile; and exile, in the metaphorical love story lens, is like Israel being thrust out of the house (cf. Deut 6:19; 9:4), or being driven out of the land (cf. Exod 23:28–31; 33:2; 34:11; Num 32:51–56; Deut 11:23) by the LORD God.[11] God has the prerogative to banish his brazenly unfaithful bride because God is the homeowner, so to speak; or, as another analogy in Scripture puts it, God says, "The land is mine; with me you are but aliens and tenants" in it (Lev 25:23 NRSV). Consequently, God repossesses the Israelites' home because of elongated covenant unfaithfulness or spiritual adultery.

An alternative view (or multivalent expression) of exile, in Scripture, views the covenant partners not as completely separated and estranged. Ezekiel receives a series of visions wherein God's presence leaves Jerusalem and the land of Judah to go eastward into Babylonia, the land of captivity (Ezek 10–11); thus, in a sense, God goes with the Judahites into exile—even goes before them (cf. Ezek 1). Inversely, Isaiah prophecies that God will lead the Judean exiles back to the promised land after the period of exile, as a second exodus (Isa 43), which presumes God is with them from that starting point in Babylon. As a result, even in the darkest moments God is near.

4.5 Hopes for Reconciliation

The divorce concept is quite grave, and indeed exile is perhaps the darkest period in the life of Israel and salvation history; yet, there are glimmers of hope in Scripture notwithstanding concerning life beyond exile. Often part and parcel of the same prophetic messages that pronounce the covenant broken (or of metaphorical divorce) and the impending exile (or of being thrown out of the house) also contain messages of returning to the land and prospects of a new covenant for the exiles, the Jewish remnant. Relational

---

11. These scriptural citations refer to God evicting the Canaanites, not the Israelites; nevertheless, the reason for the Canaanites' and Israelites' expulsion from the land is for the same reason: a great sin debt due to idolatry. This expulsion is also vividly conceptualized as the land vomiting out its inhabitants (Lev 18:25–28).

reconciliation is, therefore, in view not only as a possible reality but a foretold one.

4.5.1 Returning to the Land

Though the divorce metaphor is utilized in Jeremiah and Isaiah, Scripture is often multivalent; accordingly, at times the exile is otherwise depicted as an estrangement, that is, a period of separation after which there is reconciliation and restoration (cf. Ezek 36:16-38). This notion is perceived in God's foretelling of the remnants' return to the land after exile (see Jer 29:10-14; 30:10-11; 31:7-9; 32:36-41; cf. also Ezek 37). For example, God proclaims,

> See, I am going to gather them from all the lands to which I drove them in my anger and my wrath and in great indignation; I will bring them back to this place, and I will settle them in safety. They shall be my people, and I will be their God. I will give them one heart and one way, that they may fear me for all time, for their own good and the good of their children after them. . . . I will rejoice in doing good to them, and I will plant them in this land in faithfulness, with all my heart and all my soul. (Jer 32:37-39, 41 NRSV)

The literal returning to the promised land after a seventy-year exile is metaphorically akin to God, who had formerly kicked his unfaithful wife out of the house, as allowing his estrange spouse to move back in with him in their home. Naturally, if an estranged couple resumes cohabitation, then reconciliatory efforts are in place and engaged. These are hopeful circumstances.

4.5.2 A New Covenant

In addition to the implied relational reconciliation in the gesture of the Israelites returning to the promised land, God makes explicit promises of a new future together in terms of a forthcoming new covenant. If covenant is like marriage and a broken covenant is like a divorce, then prospects of a new covenant is metaphorically analogous to a remarriage (see further ch. 5). There are two significant prophecies regarding God's promise of a new covenant or a remarriage, namely Hos 2 and Jer 31–32; supplementary references indicate that this forthcoming new covenant will be an everlasting covenant (cf. Isa 55:3; 61:8; Jer 32:40; 50:5; Ezek 16:60; 37:26; cf. also Heb 13:20).[12]

In Hosea, sandwiched between the analogy of covenant unfaithfulness as spiritual adultery, God already foresees a remedy to the current dilemma in the form of a new covenant. God declares, "I will make for you a covenant on that day. . . . And I will take you for my wife forever; I will take you for my wife in righteousness and in justice, in steadfast love, and in mercy. I will take you for my wife in faithfulness; and you shall know the LORD" (Hos 2:18–20 NRSV). Speaking of a covenant at a future date implies a new covenant; further, the verbiage of *betrothal* (so, e.g., ESV) indicates starting the relationship over again. Moshe Weinfeld explicates, "God espouses (again) his bride (Israel), and he gives her for dowry the virtues: righteousness, justice, grace, mercy and faith, and by means of it he reunites himself with the bride."[13]

Jeremiah, who prophesied of spiritual unfaithfulness and divorce, is also the prophet who holds out hope of restoration in the context of a new marriage/covenant. God foretells,

> The days are surely coming, says the LORD, when I will make a new covenant with the house of Israel and the house of Judah. It will not be like the covenant that I made with their ancestors when I took them by the hand to bring them out of the land of Egypt—a covenant that they broke, though I was their husband, says the LORD. But this is the covenant that I will make with the house of Israel after those days, says the LORD: I will put my law within them, and I will write it on their hearts; and I will

---

12. Other everlasting covenants include the one with Noah, promising no more catastrophic floods (Gen 9:16); the one with Abraham promising land and descendants (Gen 17:7, 13, 19; Ps 105:10–11; 1 Chr 16:17–18); the one with David, promising a never-ending dynasty (2 Sam 23:5).

13. Weinfeld, "Imagery of God," 523.

Divorce

be their God, and they shall be my people. (Jer 31:31–33 NRSV)

This prophetic oracle carries the literal and figurative meanings the soundest. God, as a husband, wooed his bride by rescuing that damsel in distress (slavery in Egypt); or, God, as covenant partner, rectifying the initial covenant seeks to make a new covenant which will enable the Israelites to meet its requirements. Hope is not lost.

4.6 Trying to Observe a Broken Covenant, or Participate in an Annulled Marriage?

Whereupon the Persian king Cyrus liberated all previously exiled peoples in captivity under the Babylonian Empire, the Jewish remnant returns to their homeland (Judah/Judaea/Yehud) in order to resettle their cities and rebuild their entire society. Over the course of several years, houses were constructed (Hag 1), the temple was rebuilt (Ezra 3), and the holistic socioreligious economy which the Israelites had previously known was beginning to materialize again (cf. Ezra 6; Neh 8; Hag 2; Zech 4–5; Mal 1–2). Hopes were high that the Mosaic/Sinaitic covenantal ideal could be actualized in this new era.

The Jewish exiles knew that by suffering captivity and exile they had hitherto paid for their accrued sins of covenantal unfaithfulness (Lam 4:22a; cf. also Isa 40:1–2; Jer 16:18). Therefore, there was a fresh start after exile, and the returnees did not want to make the same errors again; rather, there was a dogged determination on the part of the Yehudite leadership to be loyal to God's (Mosaic/Sinaitic) covenant in every regard (cf. Ezra 9–10; Neh 5, 8, 13; cf. also Hag 1; Mal 1–2).[14]

However, the question must be asked: if the (literal) exile indicates a (metaphoric) divorce, due to the (figurative) breaking of the covenant, then are the returnees' efforts in keeping covenant

---

14. All the activity of these cited chapters directly flows out of the covenantal obligations, as per Deuteronomy.

futile? Posed differently: is the Jewish remnant trying to adhere to a marriage covenant that's been nullified? On the one hand, the postexilic minor prophets speak as though the law, the Mosaic/Sinaitic Covenant, is still binding. On the other hand, the postexilic books of Ezra and Nehemiah emit a sense of one-sided effort, by the remnant (elite) making their own covenants (Ezra 10:3; cf. Neh 9:38). Irrespectively, there is truth, morality, and ethics contained in the law—e.g., the timeless Ten Commandments—so it can only be good to continue in these dictums; and, there was some cognition that the Mosaic/Sinaitic Covenant was an eternal one, so long as its commandments were obeyed (cf. Neh 1:5; 9:8, 32; 13:2).[15]

This quandary will be suspended for the moment. More implications and repercussions emit from the notion of a new covenant, and this will be developed further in the next chapter (ch. 5). Indeed, the story of God's love continues . . . into the New Testament!

---

15. Cf. Dumbrell, *Covenant and Creation*, 153–62.

Excursus D

Ring Off—Ring On

THE WEDDING RING IS perhaps the most iconic symbol denoting the status of one in a marriage relationship. In wedding ceremonies commentary is usually given on the ring's symbolic significance. Often the geometric aspect of the ring is highlighted: just as a circle has no beginning and no end, so may your love be ongoing in God's eternal love and faithfulness. Or, the location of the wedding ring is underscored: the so-called ring finger is the only digit to have a vein which connects to the heart—the *vena amoris*, vein of love. Indeed, the ring is truly an idealized symbol.

Periodically my wife, Julie, will leave her wedding ring in the bathroom. Having removed it for a shower, she sometime forgets to put it back on after the morning preparation routine is complete. When I find her heirloom wedding ring by the bathroom sink, I return it to her; I put the ring on Julie's finger and jestingly say: Will you stay married to me? My feeble attempt at humor erroneously identifies the marriage relationship to be in existence only when the ring is on her finger.

In Scripture, a figurative ring comes into focus during the postexilic era and its associated oracles make sense both of the contemporary time frame of the remnant community and the end of the monarchic period. By examining Hag 2 and retrospectively interpreting Jer 22, God's metaphoric wedding ring plays an important role in conveying God's loving disposition before the end of the kingdoms of Israel and Judah, and during the postexilic era. In short, the once severed or estranged relationship between the Israelites and God turns to restoration and reconciliation, all figuratively denoted by the prophets in terms of God's signet (wedding) ring.

1. Zerubbabel (Hag 2) & Jehoiachin (Jer 22)

After the Babylonian Empire was overthrown, King Cyrus of Persia in his first year of ruling the expanded empire liberated all previously captured people groups, including the Judeans/Jewish peoples (Ezra 1:1–4; see also 2 Chr 36:22–23; cf. Isa 44:28–45:6, 13; 48:14–15). The Jewish remnant returned to Judaea/Yehud to rebuild the temple in Jerusalem and reestablish the national community in conformity with the law of the LORD. The books of Ezra and Nehemiah, Zechariah and Haggai all relate the restoration of national identity, with a renewed fervor for covenant faithfulness (cf. ch. 4).

In this setting, God speaks through the prophet Haggai addressing Zerubbabel, who is the governor of Judaea/Yehud, province of the Persian Empire. In the following oracle, mention is made of a signet ring, or metaphorically a wedding ring, which is part of a larger motif in Scripture.

> The word of the LORD came a second time to Haggai on the twenty-fourth day of the month: Speak to Zerubbabel, governor of Judah, saying, I am about to shake the heavens and the earth, and to overthrow the throne of kingdoms; I am about to destroy the strength of the kingdoms of the nations, and overthrow the chariots and their riders; and the horses and their riders shall fall, every one by the sword of a comrade. On that day, says the LORD of hosts, I will take you, O Zerubbabel my servant, son of Shealtiel, says the LORD, and make you like a signet ring; for I have chosen you, says the LORD of hosts. (Hag 2:20–23 NRSV)

The reference to Zerubbabel as God's signet ring primarily connotes authority in leadership, yet the ring is evocative of

Ring Off—Ring On

covenantal relationship, as a wedding ring placed back onto the representative bride's finger. This ring placed back on the finger implies that it had been previously removed. Jeremiah relates this ring removal in the following oracle.

> As I live, says the LORD, even if King Coniah son of Jehoiakim of Judah were the signet ring on my right hand, even from there I would tear you off and give you into the hands of those who seek your life, into the hands of those of whom you are afraid, even into the hands of King Nebuchadrezzar of Babylon and into the hands of the Chaldeans. I will hurl you and the mother who bore you into another country, where you were not born, and there you shall die. But they shall not return to the land to which they long to return. Is this man Coniah a despised broken pot, a vessel no one wants? Why are he and his offspring hurled out and cast away in a land that they do not know? O land, land, land, hear the word of the LORD! Thus says the LORD: Record this man as childless, a man who shall not succeed in his days; for none of his offspring shall succeed in sitting on the throne of David, and ruling again in Judah. (Jer 22:24-30 NRSV; cf. Jer 27:20)

When taken together, Jer 22 speaks of God's removal of the kingship, as a (marriage) ring, and the replacement of God's political leader in Hag 2, as a (marriage) ring. Further, 1 Chr 3 explicates how Zerubbabel is Jehoiachin's (or *Coniah* for short) direct descendant; so, this is the resumption of the kingly line of David, insofar as possible.[1] Therefore, the exilic period of seventy years is, through this imagery, a marital estrangement at the least or a divorce at the most (see ch. 4)—and all symbolized by a wedding or signet ring.

A few extrapolations can be retrospectively made based on these two texts referring to a signet ring. First, it can be deduced that David was the initial recipient of this figurative wedding ring;

---

1. Note that in the postexilic era of the Persian period the highest political leader was a governor of a province, not a king, since the emperor ruled over all provinces (cf. Esth 1:1-2).

if at exile the ring comes off of the last king of Judah, then the ring must have went on the first king to whom God made a covenant regarding an eternal Davidic dynasty (2 Sam 7). Though the united monarchy divides with Solomon's son Rehoboam, the Jerusalem throne of Judah retains the promises of the Davidic Covenant. Second, Zerubbabel was only the first of the Davidic governors of Judaea/Yehud from whom the hopes of the messiah would eventually source (Jer 23:5; 33:15; cf. Zech 3:8; 6:12). Third, apparently God's promise of an everlasting Davidic dynasty is not broken by the exile, but suspended.

2. Jesus in the New Testament

If the Davidic kings were God's wedding ring, as it were, for God's bride, then Jesus might be metaphorically viewed as God's own wedding ring, which God wears to express God's own commitment, fidelity, and love. Within this metaphorical wedding ring motif, the New Testament shows Jesus both as a figurative signet ring and the ultimate Davidic king who reigns eternally (cf. 2 Sam 7:13, 16). In this complex expression, God becoming flesh in Jesus fulfills the mystical (marital) union for both the duration (everlasting) and extent (royalty [cf. Exod 19:6; 1 Pet 2:5–9; Rev 1:6; 5:10; 20:6]) to which God intends for the marriage.

The signet ring functioned as an authoritative seal imprinting the crest upon paper, with wax.[2] The imprinting concept is somewhat resonant of a verse in the New Testament referring to Jesus. Hebrews 1:3a (NRSV) declares, "He [Jesus] is the reflection of God's glory and the exact imprint of God's very being, and he sustains all things by his powerful word." This imprinting may be inferred as the impression of the signet ring, i.e., the authorization of God. Furthermore, it is only the resurrected and ascended Christ who is able to break open the seven seals in Rev 5; this encoded

---

2. Magness-Gardiner, "Seals, Mesopotamian," *ABD*, 5:1062–4.

imagery connotes that Jesus is the sovereign to unroll—and reign over—the rest of history.[3]

Therefore, Jesus, the son of David (e.g., Matt 1:1; Rev 5:5), was enthroned, as it were, on the cross.[4] After his resurrection, Jesus ascended on high to the right hand of God Almighty (John 3:13; 6:62; 20:17; Acts 2:29-35; Rom 10:5-13; Eph 4:8-10). This all ensures that God's marital, or (new) covenantal, commitment will remain to the utmost degree for all of eternity, since Jesus is fully human and fully God and, as such, lives forever, resulting in an everlasting, unbreakable marriage covenant (see further ch. 5).

---

3. Roloff, *Revelation of John*, 75-78.
4. Wright, *How God Became King*, 227.

5

(Re)Marriage

5.1 Marriage (Again)

THIS CHAPTER IS ENTITLED "(Re)Marriage" with the parenthetical prefix because of perspective and recipient. As will be demonstrated, the new covenant which Jesus inaugurates and envelopes people into is both for the Jew and the Gentile (see, e.g., Rom 1:16). Thus, the salvation-relationship of the new covenant is a *remarriage* for the Jews (or Hebrews/Israelites), yet for the Gentile this is the first and only *marriage* invitation made available to them.[1]

To exemplify this concept, the movie *The Parent Trap* serves as a working illustration. This film, originally produced in 1961 starring Hayley Mills and its remake in 1998 starring Lindsay Lohan, tells the fictional story of a set of parents who had divorced when their twin daughters were very young, each parent taking one child. Years later, as teenagers, these twins attend the same summer camp, meet each other, and learn of their common origin. At the end of the summer the girls switch places to live with the opposite parent; and their plan is to reunite the parents so the family can all live together. Over the course of the film this indeed

---

1. Notwithstanding, in ancient Israel (as depicted in the Old Testament) foreign persons were able to be integrated into its life and religion; cf. Ruppert, "Foreigners in the Old and New Testaments," 151–63.

transpires; the father and mother are subsequently remarried, and the family becomes reunited.

In *The Parent Trap*, the parents technically become remarried, entering into marriage with their original partners; this is like God remarrying the Hebrew/Israelite/Jewish people.[2] In another sense, though, the parents' marital union later in life is new, with new or modified circumstances and conditions mostly because of the children, the larger family unit. This is like God marrying the Gentile (non-Jewish) peoples in the new covenant with Jesus as the bridegroom.

Thus, in the (re)marriage stage of God's love story, God—in Jesus—enters (again) into a marriage-like covenant with a chosen people.[3] The final part of God's love story, moreover, is the time frame in which we find ourselves, for in between Jesus' two advents (his birth and return), is the era of the church. Consequently, the eternal and abundant salvation-relationship, or marriage (new) covenant, is available for those who will be saved.

5.2 A New Covenant

In the Old Testament, even before the kingdoms of the Israelites were exiled, God already foretold the coming of a new covenant (see ch. 4). A new covenant is never realized in the remaining Old Testament canon, however. So, when does that prophesied new covenant actualize? One must look farther into the second temple period, read into the New Testament to Jesus' last day until mention is made of a new covenant which Jesus inaugurates!

---

2. In chapter 1 (n2), it was indicated that the Hebrew people become known as *Israelites* when they proliferate. Likewise, the *Jewish people* (or *Jews*) is a synonymous term for the same group of people during the postexilic era of the Old and New Testaments.

3. For scriptural undergirding of remarriage, see, e.g., Adams, *Marriage, Divorce, and Remarriage*; Instone-Brewer, *Divorce and Remarriage*. Cf. also House, *Divorce and Remarriage*.

5.2.1 The New Covenant in the Old Testament

In order to appreciate the significance of Jesus' new covenant, juxtaposing examination of Jer 31 and the Gospel accounts must be undertaken. This new covenant was foretold several hundred years before it came to pass by prophets such as Jeremiah. Jeremiah 31:31–34 (NRSV) reads:

> The days are surely coming, says the LORD, when I will make a new covenant with the house of Israel and the house of Judah. It will not be like the covenant that I made with their ancestors when I took them by the hand to bring them out of the land of Egypt—a covenant that they broke, though I was their husband, says the LORD. But this is the covenant that I will make with the house of Israel after those days, says the LORD: I will put my law within them, and I will write it on their hearts; and I will be their God, and they shall be my people. No longer shall they teach one another, or say to each other, "Know the LORD," for they shall all know me, from the least of them to the greatest, says the LORD; for I will forgive their iniquity, and remember their sin no more. (cf. Hos 2:18–20)

What is curious about this most extensive Old Testament passage related to new covenant is the different kind of lawgiving ("I will put my law within them, and I will write it on their heart") and the actualization of forgiveness of sins ("I will forgive their iniquity, and remember their sin no more"). Ezekiel, relatedly, prophecies similarly:

> I will sprinkle clean water upon you, and you shall be clean from all your uncleannesses, and from all your idols I will cleanse you. A new heart I will give you, and a new spirit I will put within you; and I will remove from your body the heart of stone and give you a heart of flesh. I will put my spirit within you, and make you follow my statutes and be careful to observe my ordinances. (Ezek 36:25–27 NRSV)

(Re)Marriage

Taking these two passages together, a composite picture emerges. Instead of the Ten Commandments chiseled on tablets of stone, the new covenant commandments will be imprinted on new types of human hearts, ones tenderized by the Spirit of God (cf. 2 Cor 3). Further, it is the transformed heart and the indwelling Spirit of God within the new covenant partner which allows the adherent to obey, to be faithful to the new covenant commandments and teach others the same. These new circumstances facilitate a new result; the result is that God and the new kind of human are spouses in an eternal marriage covenant relationship (Ezek 36:28; cf. Jer 31:32b). These are the attributes to be anticipated when reading the New Testament.

5.2.2 The New Covenant in the New Testament

The four Gospel accounts tell of the good news of God in the life of Jesus the Christ/Messiah and Savior. Though spending his entire public career declaring and demonstrating the kingdom of God, Jesus only makes a few references to a new covenant and only at the very end of his life which he inaugurates, along with the kingdom of God, by his death and resurrection. Specifically, Jesus makes new covenant statements when observing Passover with his disciples for the last time.

Midway through the lengthy and didactic Passover meal, which commemorates Israel's original and archetypal salvation experience[4]—the exodus from slavery in Egypt—Jesus "took a loaf of bread, and when he had given thanks, he broke it and gave it to them, saying, 'This is my body, which is given for you. Do this in remembrance of me.' And he did the same with the cup after supper, saying, 'This cup that is poured out for you is the new covenant in my blood'" (Luke 22:19–20 NRSV; cf. 1 Cor 11:23–25). Of all the menu items comprising the Passover meal,[5] Jesus reinterprets the bread of affliction (of three loaves of bread) and the cup

---

4. Levenson (*Resurrection and the Restoration of Israel*, 27) declares: "The exodus has become a prototype of ultimate redemption."

5. See, e.g., Silverman, *Passover Haggadah*.

of redemption (of four cups of wine) as analogous of his very self and his forthcoming salvific achievement.[6] Therefore, the events in the upper room with Jesus and his disciples is a (new) covenant ratifying ceremony.[7]

But why is it necessary for Jesus Christ to die in order to inaugurate the new covenant, the (re)new(ed) marriage? Several doctrinal answers could be given, yet within the metaphorical love story lens something very interesting emerges. Covenants were always ratified with blood; blood was essentially the notarization of covenants. We saw the Mosaic/Sinaitic Covenant ratified by the sprinkling of bulls' blood (Exod 24:7–8). Now, since that blood came from a finite animal the (marriage) covenant is therefore temporal; however, during the second marriage-like ceremony between God and humanity Jesus says he will offer his own blood. The significance being since Jesus, the Son and Christ of God, is an infinite and living Savior his blood of his (marriage) covenant is an eternal one (Heb 9).[8]

The author of Hebrews, interpreting Jer 31 in light of Jesus in the Gospels, surmises that "in speaking of 'a new covenant,' he [Jesus] has made the first one obsolete" (Heb 8:13 NRSV). Significantly, Jesus—as fully human and fully divine—serves as both parties: as (the Son of) God and as the human mediator of the new covenant (Heb 9:15; 12:24). The failure of the Mosaic/Sinaitic Covenant could perhaps be distilled to the fact that one covenant partner was divine and the other human (collective Israel); alternatively, in the new covenant—while there is still a human covenant partner (collective salvation recipients) and a divine one (Christ/Messiah)—the divine new covenant partner also shares in humanity by taking on flesh as Jesus, and the human new covenant partner similarly shares in divinity by being regenerated and indwelled

---

6. See further, Jeremias, *Eucharistic Words*.

7. As mentioned in "Excursus B," the sign of the new covenant or the vow renewal ceremony for the new covenant is the eucharistic meal, where the body/bread and blood/wine of Christ is regularly ingested and imbibed, shared and realized.

8. "Wine, described in biblical texts as the blood of grapes, can have a symbolic meaning as blood" (Carmichael, "Eucharist and the Passover Seder," 66).

(Re)Marriage

by the Holy Spirit. Consequently, the investment or endowment of both parties enables empathy and empowers fidelity within the covenant relationship (cf. "Excursus C").

All human new covenant partners are those whose sins are forgiven by means of Jesus' perfect substitutionary sacrifice, receiving Jesus' resurrection life; and this is all garnered by the individual's faith in Christ Jesus activated by the grace of God (Eph 2:9–10; cf. Rom 10:9–10). Therefore, instead of new covenant partners only comprised of those in the upper room the day before Jesus' death, new covenant partners are all future recipients of God's grace unto new life (cf. John 17:20). Just as one is included into God's new covenant by means of redemption and reconciliation, so too human new covenant partners may envelop other people into salvation, marriage-like relationship as "ministers of a new covenant" (2 Cor 3:6 NRSV), "ambassadors for Christ" entrusted with "the ministry of reconciliation" (2 Cor 5:20, 18 NRSV)!

5.2.3 The New Covenant Commandment(s)

Like the Mosaic/Sinaitic Covenant, the new covenant has commandments, which have been likened to metaphorical marital terms (see ch. 2). Unlike the Mosaic/Sinaitic Covenant, though, with its 613 total commandments and governing Ten Commandments, Jesus has precisely *one* marital term, i.e., one new covenant commandment. In the context of the Last Supper or covenant ceremony (see above), Jesus states, "I give you a new commandment, that you love one another. Just as I have loved you, you also should love one another" (John 13:34 NRSV; cf. 2 John 5). To reiterate, this new (and only) commandment is the entire legislation for the new covenant; however, it does not sound entirely new.

The greatest commandment is the *Shema* (Matt 22:34–40 // Mark 12:28–29; cf. Luke 10:25–28): "Hear, O Israel: The LORD is our God, the LORD alone. You shall love the LORD your God with all your heart, and with all your soul, and with all your might" (Deut 6:4–5 NRSV). Jesus always paired this first commandment with the second one like it: "You shall love your neighbor as yourself" (Lev 19:18b NRSV; cf. Mark 12:31). Thus, Jesus merges loving God and loving people into one throughout his life and ministry; and doing the same for the "new commandment" of the new covenant, Jesus also qualifies the extent, defines the degree to which that love must be demonstrated:[9] "as I have loved you" (John 13:34; cf. John 3:16; 15:13-14; 1 John 3:16). Jesus set himself as the standard because he has fulfilled the law (Matt 5:17-20), thereby becoming the embodiment of the law.

Reflecting again on the metaphorical meaning of the new commandment as the marital term of the marriage-like covenant relationship, this love vow, while singular, is all-encompassing. If the synoptic gospels (particularly Luke) are harmonized with the Gospel of John (see above), then it is in the context of the (re)marriage (or new covenant) ceremony where Jesus and his disciples exchange their marital vow (or new commandment); in addition, it is significant that these actions take place in the setting of a religious festival (Passover), evoking a wedding banquet. In fact, nearly every action that took place in the upper room parallels a traditional Jewish wedding; not only are these parallels striking, they will also advance the (re)marriage metaphor for new covenant partners to illuminate salvation in Jesus as a marriage-like relationship with the Living God.

5.2.4 Jewish Wedding Ceremonies

About halfway into a traditional Jewish wedding the following three parts are the centerpiece of the ceremony. The first part is as follows: "The two betrothal blessings, one over wine and one over the act of betrothal that will follow, are recited by a rabbi. The rabbi does not drink the wine, but gives the goblet to the groom and then to the bride, for each to take a sip."[10] Once they sip the wine, the couple's first betrothal blessing is complete; the second betrothal blessing comes the moment when "the groom places a ring on the

---

9. McKnight, *Jesus Creed*, 20-22.
10. Greenberg, "Marriage in the Jewish Tradition," 10.

bride's right index finger and recites the ancient declaration, 'Behold, thou art consecrated unto me, according to the laws of Moses and of Israel.' Her acceptance of the ring is considered assent."[11] Next, in the second part, "the marriage contract is read aloud in its original Aramaic."[12] The third "part of the ceremony consists of seven different blessings of celebration and hope. Customarily, seven different guests are given the honor, each reciting one blessing. The seventh blessing is as follows:

> Blessed art Thou, Lord our God, creator of the universe Who has created joy and gladness, bridegroom and bride, laughter and exultation, pleasure and delight, love, brotherhood, peace, and fellowship. May it be soon, O Lord our God, that there be heard in the cities of Judah and in the streets of Jerusalem the voice of joy and gladness, the voice of bridegroom and of bride, the jubilant voice of bridegrooms from their canopies and of youths from their feasts of song. Blessed art Thou, O Lord, Who enables bridegroom to rejoice with the bride.

Upon completion of the blessings, of which the first is the benediction over wine, the couple drinks from the wine goblet."[13]

In summation, the centerpiece of a traditional Jewish wedding has the following components: (1) blessings with a cup of wine; (2) the marriage contract; (3) blessings with a cup of wine. This marriage custom appears to be Luke's literary design, in form and content, when conveying the Last Supper events; for, whereas Matthew (Matt 26:27-28) and Mark (Mark 14:23-24) narrate one cup and make mention of a covenant, Luke highlights two cups in his account and explicitly states it to be a *new* covenant (Luke 22:17-20). Consequently, Jesus' marriage-like contract with his disciples, in between two blessings with a goblet of wine each, is to share in the resurrection life of Jesus in the kingdom of God (Luke 22:18b-19);[14] also, the Eucharist, or Communion, may be seen as

---

11. Greenberg, "Marriage in the Jewish Tradition," 10.
12. Greenberg, "Marriage in the Jewish Tradition," 10.
13. Greenberg, "Marriage in the Jewish Tradition," 10-11.
14. Cf. Evans, *Luke*, 317. Jeremias, *Eucharistic Words*, 166-72.

the anticipation of the fulfillment of the kingdom of God in the form of the eternal (wedding) banquet (see further 5.5).[15]

5.3 Free to Remarry?

Whereas divorce was permitted in the law (see ch. 4), the prospect of remarriage was much more complicated; and while both the biblical legislation of divorce and remarriage is somewhat ambiguous in terms of a unified and integrated application,[16] a few aspects are clear. According to Deut 22:22-24 the spouse who has an extramarital affair must die (cf. Matt 19:7-9); and, according to Deut 24:1-4 the husband who remarries his divorced wife (who had married another man in the interim) must die (cf. Hos 3). This has an intriguing theological counterpart in the new covenant. Jesus, the Son of God, *died* in order to *remarry* Jews who would be disciples of Christ (as well as marry Gentile disciples of Christ); and, both Jews and Gentiles who receive Jesus' salvation must first acknowledge that they are *dead* because of sin (Rom 3:23; 6:23), and sinning is metaphorically committing a *spiritual affair* against God (see ch. 3). In fact, those regenerated by the Holy Spirit unto salvation-relationship with the Son and Savior are called to daily spiritually die to the unregenerate self and live the new creation life of Christ (see Luke 9:23-24; Rom 6; 8; 12:1-2; 1 Cor 15:21-22; 2 Cor 5:17). Consequently, death is the mechanism of marriage annulment and death is the mechanism for remarriage, as per the love story of God (see Rom 7:1-6).

5.4 Jesus as Bridegroom and the Church as Bride

In the Gospels, Jesus implies through a parabolic teaching that he himself is a bridegroom, which justifies the feasting (versus fasting) activity in which Jesus and his disciples regularly participate (Matt 9:15 // Mark 2:19-20 // Luke 5:34-35). On another occasion,

---

15. Marshall, *Luke*, 799.
16. Cf. Wenham and Heth, *Jesus and Divorce*.

(RE)MARRIAGE

the bridegroom figure is attributed to Jesus by John the Baptizer, as John indicates that the bride (those being saved) is not his, but Jesus' bride; rather, John is the humble and joyous best man, as it were (John 3:28-30).[17] Jesus as bridegroom might also be implicitly conveyed when Jesus performs his first miracle in the setting of a wedding banquet (John 2:1-10), which is portentous of his passion;[18] and a couple of Jesus' parables are also set in the context of a wedding reception (Matt 22:1-14 // Luke 14:15-24; Matt 25:1-13).[19] Additionally, it is provocative that in the same passage which details the messianic manifesto (Isa 61:1-2a, quoted in Luke 4:18-19), which Jesus reads in the synagogue and pronounces its simultaneous fulfillment, later foretells the protagonist (i.e., Jesus) figuratively clothed by the LORD God as a bride and groom (Isa 61:10; cf. also Isa 49:18; 62:5).

In the Epistles more explicit reference is made of not only Jesus being the bridegroom but also the bride of Christ being the church, that is the collection of all individuals who have received salvation by grace through faith in Christ Jesus.[20] Ephesians 5 is renowned for its wedding imagery between Jesus as bridegroom and the church as bride (see also 2 Cor 11:2; cf. Rom 7:1-6)—and often this text is appropriated in contemporary wedding ceremonies as the biblical schema by which to understand the joining together of a Christian husband and wife. The key passage reads:

> Be subject to one another out of reverence for Christ. Wives, be subject to your husbands as you are to the Lord. For the husband is the head of the wife just as Christ is the head of the church, the body of which he is the Savior. Just as the church is subject to Christ, so also wives ought to be, in everything, to their husbands. Husbands,

---

17. Jeremias, "νύμφη, νυμφίος," *TDNT*, 4:1101, 1104.

18. Note Jesus' expression, in the Fourth Gospel, of how his/the hour has not yet come, is coming, and has come (John 2:4; 4:21, 23; 5:25, 28; 7:30; 8:20; 12:23, 27; 13:1; 16:2, 4, 21, 25, 32; 17:1)—and the eschatological reverberations thereof.

19. Jeremias, "νύμφη, νυμφίος," *TDNT*, 4:1100-4.

20. Reddish, "Bride of Christ," *ABD*, 1:782; Jeremias, "νύμφη, νυμφίος," *TDNT*, 4:1104-6.

love your wives, just as Christ loved the church and gave himself up for her, in order to make her holy by cleansing her with the washing of water by the word, so as to present the church to himself in splendor, without a spot or wrinkle or anything of the kind—yes, so that she may be holy and without blemish. In the same way, husbands should love their wives as they do their own bodies. He who loves his wife loves himself. For no one ever hates his own body, but he nourishes and tenderly cares for it, just as Christ does for the church, because we are members of his body. "For this reason a man will leave his father and mother and be joined to his wife, and the two will become one flesh." This is a great mystery, and I am applying it to Christ and the church. Each of you, however, should love his wife as himself, and a wife should respect her husband. (Eph 5:21–33 NRSV)

Verse 21 is crucial for proper interpretation—*every* Christian is to subject, or *submit* (NIV), oneself "to one another out of reverence for Christ" (Eph 5:21 NRSV). In the context of marriage, what this looks like for the husband is primarily loving his wife (Eph 5:33a)—even sacrificially, ala Jesus (Eph 5:25); and what this looks like for the wife is to respect her husband (Eph 5:33b), which is an appropriate response to Christ-like love. While the text does say the woman/wife should be in *submission* to her husband (Eph 5:22–24), every male/husband is also in *subjection* to his Heavenly Spouse (see Eph 1:22; cf. also Eph 6:9)!

Thus, the marriage relationship of a Christian husband and wife (Eph 5:33) is to reveal and reenact Jesus' self-sacrificing, generous-giving love for humanity—and the continual acceptance of said love. "Marriage is a significant allegory" (Eph 5:32a CEB), therefore, purporting to the "profound mystery" (Eph 5:32 NIV) of the union which exists between "Christ and the church" (Eph 5:32b NRSV).[21] This mystical union is further elaborated in Revelation; there the remaining references to bridegroom and bride,

---

21. Ortlund, *Marriage and the Mystery of the Gospel*.

as well as the associated developments in the wedding imagery and marriage relationship, are fully developed.[22]

5.5 The New Jerusalem as the Bride of Christ

The marriage ceremony of the new covenant is unique in that as opposed to it taking place on one day, the invitation and wedding procedures have been happening for thousands of years and will continue to recur until Jesus makes his second advent. Indeed, salvation is offered and available from the time of Jesus' resurrection until the time of his return to earth. In that long marriage ceremony, as it were, the number of the collective bride increases until Jesus brings her home (cf. John 14:2–3). Revelation 21 provides a glimpse of the bride of Christ.

> Then I saw a new heaven and a new earth; for the first heaven and the first earth had passed away, and the sea was no more. And I saw the holy city, the new Jerusalem, coming down out of heaven from God, prepared as a bride adorned for her husband. And I heard a loud voice from the throne saying, "See, the home of God is among mortals. He will dwell with them; they will be his peoples, and God himself will be with them; he will wipe every tear from their eyes. Death will be no more; mourning and crying and pain will be no more, for the first things have passed away." And the one who was seated on the throne said, "See, I am making all things new." . . . Then one of the seven angels who had the seven bowls full of the seven last plagues came and said to me, "Come, I will show you the bride, the wife of the Lamb." And in the spirit he carried me away to a great, high mountain and showed me the holy city Jerusalem coming down out of heaven from God. (Rev 21:1–5a, 9–10 NRSV)

Revelation is apocalyptic literature, which means it is highly encoded in symbolism, imagery, and numerology;[23] consequent-

22. Smolarz, *Covenant and the Metaphor of Divine Marriage*.
23. For excellent exegesis of Revelation, see Beale, *Revelation*, esp. here 50–69.

ly, interpretation is at times difficult. Fortunately, in the text above the figurative language is internally decoded, yielding a straightforward message.

The bride of Christ (Rev 21:2b, 9b) is metaphorically portrayed as and equated with the New Jerusalem (Rev 21:2a, 10a). This figurative city is a cubic structure (Rev 21:16), evoking the only other cubic structure in Scripture: the temple's holy of holies (1 Kgs 6:10a), set in Jerusalem. Further, the ornamentation of the eschatological city (bride) has many of its precious stones in common with the high priests' medallion (Exod 28:15–21, 39:8–14). This indicates the bride of Christ (the New Jerusalem) has a priestly aspect to her; indeed, she is the total priesthood of all believers (Rev 1:5–6; 5:9–10; 20:6; 1 Pet 2:4–5; cf. Exod 19:6).

The bride of Christ descends from heaven to earth (Rev 21:2, 10b)—like a bride walking down the aisle—to be united to her groom. The marital oneness is expressed through "a reciprocal covenant promise which is ultimately patterned after Near Eastern marriage contracts, 'and they shall be his people[s], and God himself shall be with them [and be their God]'"[24] (see Rev 21:3; cf. Jer 24:7; 31:33; 32:38; Ezek 11:20; 14:11; 37:27; Zech 8:8; contra Hos 2:2). Just as God had ushered Israel to their residence of the promised land after the Sinai wedding (see ch. 2), so Jesus creates a new residence of the new heavens and new earth for himself and the wife of the Lamb to enjoy together forever in righteousness (Rev 21:1; see also Isa 65:17; 66:22; 2 Pet 3:13).

5.6 The Eternal Wedding Banquet

Like the marriage ceremony lasting exceptionally long (see 5.5 above), the wedding reception is also extremely elongated—in fact, the wedding reception of the new covenant will never end. There's nothing like the crescendo of one's own wedding, the ceremony and reception; likewise, God has designed God's second wedding ceremony and reception to perpetually linger on a high note so

---

24. Fekkes, "His Bride Has Prepared Herself," 283. Brackets (and bracketed text) original.

(Re)Marriage

that it will never decline from the climax (this too is figurative). We catch a glimpse and foretaste into this wedding reception, or wedding banquet, in Rev 19.

> After this I heard what seemed to be the loud voice of a great multitude in heaven, saying, "Hallelujah! Salvation and glory and power to our God, for his judgments are true and just; he has judged the great whore who corrupted the earth with her fornication, and he has avenged on her the blood of his servants." Once more they said, "Hallelujah! The smoke goes up from her forever and ever." And the twenty-four elders and the four living creatures fell down and worshiped God who is seated on the throne, saying, "Amen. Hallelujah!" And from the throne came a voice saying, "Praise our God, all you his servants, and all who fear him, small and great." Then I heard what seemed to be the voice of a great multitude, like the sound of many waters and like the sound of mighty thunderpeals, crying out, "Hallelujah! For the Lord our God the Almighty reigns. Let us rejoice and exult and give him the glory, for the marriage of the Lamb has come, and his bride has made herself ready; to her it has been granted to be clothed with fine linen, bright and pure"—for the fine linen is the righteous deeds of the saints. And the angel said to me, "Write this: Blessed are those who are invited to the marriage supper of the Lamb." And he said to me, "These are true words of God." (Rev 19:1–9 NRSV)

How the groom and bride are described in this passage is very important. First, let's focus on the bridegroom. The groom, of course, is Jesus, yet he is referred to here as the *Lamb*. This moniker is used to evoke certain connotations of his personal nature and role in the world. One allusion of the name *Lamb* harkens back to the sacrificial lamb at the original Passover (Exod 12); the sacrificial lamb was killed, and its blood was smeared on the doorposts and mantel in order that the residents therein would not die but live. Another allusion of the term *Lamb* is of the suffering servant of Isa 65 who, metaphorically likened to a lamb, was prophesied as being led to the slaughter with the result of being pierced for humanity's transgressions and crushed for humanity's iniquities. A third resonance of *Lamb* is found when Jesus started his ministry and John the Baptizer declared of Jesus, "Here is the Lamb of God who takes away the sin of the world!" (John 1:29 NRSV). Jesus Christ the Lamb of God, therefore, is typified as the bridegroom in glory.

This biblical text also describes the bride of Christ, while also contrasting her with the great whore (Rev 19:2). The great whore is (another other things) an allusion to the centuries of Israel's marital unfaithfulness, her adulteries or idolatry (see ch. 3). The idolatrous persons morphs from the being a maritally unfaithful spouse in the Old Testament to the unsaved persons doomed to destruction in the New Testament. For "[God] has judged the great whore who corrupted the earth with her fornication" (Rev 19:2b NRSV), and when thrown into the lake of fire (see Rev 20:14–15) "the smoke goes up from her forever and ever" (Rev 19:3b NRSV). Hence, it is not the prostitute who will enter a marriage-like relationship with the Lamb of God; rather, it is another woman whom Jesus Christ will wed for all eternity in the new covenant.[25]

The real bride, conversely, is the saved and redeemed of humanity. The identity of the bride of Christ is the faithful, those who have come to him under his precious blood, those who have entered the new covenant through grace by faith. The bride of Christ, made righteous and faithful because of what Jesus has done for her, is depicted on what she is wearing: "to her it has been granted to be clothed with fine linen, bright and pure" (Rev 19:8a NRSV); and because Revelation is encrypted the decoding sentence to follow is: "the fine linen is the righteous deeds of the saints" (Rev 19:8b NRSV). So, the bride of Christ is beautifully adorned because she is redeemed and righteous, and she is redeemed and righteous because she is beautifully adorned.

Every wife knows that in order to pull off a wedding much preparation is involved. Not only are there preparations on a large scale, but the preparations she must undertake personally for the wedding day are also extensive: fitting into the dress, getting the

---

25. See further Huber, *Like a Bride Adorned*, 185–89.

(Re)Marriage

hair done, doing the makeup, etc. Likewise, the marriage ceremony and banquet preparations of the bride of Christ, portrayed in Revelation, are also expressed: "the marriage of the Lamb has come, and his bride has made herself ready" (Rev 19:7b NRSV). How has the bride of Christ made herself ready? The answer to this question sources from the bride's adornment.

The preparation of Jesus' bride is somewhat paradoxical, actually; for, on the one hand, "it has been *granted* to be clothed with fine linen" (Rev 19:8a NRSV, emphasis added), and on the other hand, "the fine linen is the righteous *deeds* of the saints" (Rev 19:8b NRSV, emphasis added). How can the bride's preparations be both passive (*granted*) and active (*deeds*)? The solution is found in the new terms of the new covenant: "For by grace you have been saved through faith, and this is not your own doing; it is the gift of God—not the result of works, so that no one may boast. For we are what he has made us, created in Christ Jesus for good works, which God prepared beforehand to be our way of life" (Eph 2:8–10 NRSV; cf. Jas 2:14–26). Jesus, thus, ascribes—indeed, imputes—his own righteousness upon those who believe in him as Savior and enter relationship with him as such (Rom 3:21–22; 2 Cor 5:21).

A couple biblical examples—even within the metaphor of clothing—illustrate this theological principle. In a revelatory vision to the prophet Zechariah, he saw the following.

> Then he showed me the high priest Joshua standing before the angel of the LORD, and Satan standing at his right hand to accuse him. And the LORD said to Satan, "The LORD rebuke you, O Satan! . . . Is not this man a brand plucked from the fire?" Now Joshua was dressed with filthy clothes as he stood before the angel. The angel said to those who were standing before him, "Take off his filthy clothes." And to him he said, "See, I have taken your guilt away from you, and I will clothe you with festal apparel." (Zech 3:1–4 NRSV)

Therefore, the clean clothes—symbolic of atonement of sins—were given to Joshua the high priest. The clean clothes were God's gift (cf. Isa 61:10).

Similarly, in Matt 22 Jesus told a parable of a wedding banquet. In that parable, a king prepared a wedding banquet for his son; but the original people who were invited to the wedding declined the invitation (Jews). Later the king extends another invitation to the wedding feast which was opened to anybody and everybody (Jews and Gentiles). So, people fill the banqueting hall.

> But when the king came in to see the guests, he noticed a man there who was not wearing a wedding robe, and he said to him, "Friend, how did you get in here without a wedding robe?" And he was speechless. Then the king said to the attendants, "Bind him hand and foot, and throw him into the outer darkness, where there will be weeping and gnashing of teeth."' (Matt 22:11–13 NRSV)

In the world of the parable, the king's action is extreme; however, the kingdom teaching is more sensible. Since it is unknown whether a custom existed where "the giver of a wedding feast had an obligation to provide special clothing,"[26] it is instead best to interpret the clean, "festal garment [a]s repentance."[27] Consequently, the guest with soiled clothes cannot participate in and enjoy the banquet (salvation) because he is did not first take proper measures to do so (repentance).

Therefore, Zech 3, Matt 22, and Rev 19 are all employing the same basic analogy. The opportunity for repentance and the potential for righteousness are gifts of God through Christ Jesus. If received and worn by the one who accepts it upon repentance, then that person is metaphorically the bride of Christ and literally redeemed and saved from sin and death. Indeed, the wearer of the "fine linen, bright and pure" (Rev 19:8a NRSV) "festal apparel" (Zech 3:4b NRSV) is beautiful in the sight of her groom, Jesus Christ. Therefore, "the wife of the Lamb" is "prepared as a bride adorned for her husband" (Rev 21:9b, 2b NRSV) by engaging in the good works that God has prepared in advance for the redeemed to do (Eph 2:10) as a grateful expression of salvation. This is how Jesus' "bride has made herself ready" (Rev 19:7b NRSV).

26. Albright and Mann, *Matthew*, 269 (see also 270).
27. Jeremias, *Parables of Jesus*, 188.

(Re)Marriage

5.7 Wedding Invitations

After John's revelation of the wedding banquet of the Lamb of God and the bride of Christ, "the angel said to me, 'Write this: Blessed are those who are invited to the marriage supper of the Lamb.' And he said to me, 'These are true words of God.'" (Rev 19:9 NRSV). This wedding invitation, as it were, has been written and (is being) sent to all humanity. What's more, the wedding invitation here drafted is not merely an invitation to attend, but God's invitation is to come and be involved in the wedding, to participate in the marriage supper of the Lamb of God as Jesus' spouse! The invitation is to be saved by Jesus Christ from one's sin which leads to death, to repent and accept the fine, bright, clean, and rich garments for the wedding, to accept God's free gift of salvation.

Become (part of) the bride of Christ and be wed to the loving Savior. Indeed, "Blessed are those who are invited to the marriage supper of the Lamb" (Rev 19:9 NRSV)! "The [Holy] Spirit and the bride [of Christ] say, 'Come.' And let everyone who hears say, 'Come'" (Rev 22:17a NRSV).

Excursus E

Wife-at-the-Well Type-Scene

ONE TYPE-SCENE, OUT OF many in the Bible,[1] relevant to God's love story is one that features the wife-at-the-well.[2] Type-scenes "contain a given set of repeated elements or details, not all of which are always present, not always in the same order, but enough of which are present to make the scene a recognizable one."[3] There are a few instances of the wife-at-the-well type-scene present in the Old Testament and arguably one in the New Testament.[4] The marriage arrangements in these stories cast an enriching light on God's love story as it pertains to Jesus' figurative marital union.

1. The Old Testament

The wife-at-the-well type-scenes in the Old Testament convey the fateful meeting and successive marriages of Isaac and Rebekah (Gen 24:10–28), Jacob and Rachel (Gen 29:1–12), and Moses and Zipporah (Exod 2:15–22).[5] The stories' consistent elements in the

---

1. See Alter, *Art of Biblical Narrative*, 55–78; Ska, "Our Fathers Have Told Us," 36–37.
2. Culley, *Studies in the Structure*, 41–43; Alter, *Art of Biblical Narrative*, 62–68.
3. Culley, *Studies in the Structure*, 23.
4. Williams, "The Beautiful and the Barren," 113–15.
5. Culley, *Studies in the Structure*, 41–43; Alter, *Art of Biblical Narrative*, 62–68.

Wife-at-the-Well Type-Scene

narrative are as follows. Initially, the man, who is the groom-to-be (or his representative [Gen 24]), arrives at a well after a long journey (Gen 24:10; Gen 28:10; Exod 2:15); there he meets a girl, who is always the bride-to-be. The woman is either a shepherdess come to water her flocks (Gen 29:9; Exod 2:16) or is fetching water in her jar for the household (Gen 24:15). The man usually acts cavalier in the presence of other male shepherds (Gen 29:7–10; Exod 2:17), for the woman at the well is typically reported to be beautiful (Gen 24:16a; Gen 29:17b). Once the animals are watered (Gen 24:19–20; Gen 29:10b; Exod 2:17b), the man is brought home to meet her father and family (cf. Exod 2:18–20); often the girl runs home due to her excitement (Gen 24:28; Gen 29:12b). Subsequently, marriage arrangements are made, and the man and woman are eventually wedded (Gen 24:50–67; Gen 29:14b–30; Exod 2:21–22).

Consequently, the location of the well is central to forthcoming marriages in the Old Testament. Robert Alter elucidates: "The well at an oasis is obviously a symbol of fertility.... (Proverbs 5 explicitly uses the well as a metaphor for female sexuality.) The drawing of water from the well is the act that emblematically establishes a bond—male-female, host-guest, benefactor-benefited—between the stranger and the girl."[6]

2. The New Testament

When we come to the New Testament, there is another story which appears to fit the wife-at-the-well type-scene. In John 4, Jesus approaches a well and there meets a woman; Jesus had previously sent men away (his disciples), and asks the Samarian woman, who has come to fill her water jar, for a drink of water. Up to this point, if the wife-at-the-well type-scene is set in the readers' mind, one might predict the outcome of the story based on the conventions of the narrative—are Jesus and this woman getting married?

Of the type-scene, Robert Alter maintains what is "significant is the inventive freshness with which formulas are recast and

---

6. Alter, *Art of Biblical Narrative*, 62.

redeployed in each new instance."[7] Certainly innovation is realized in John 4. Jesus and the Samaritan woman do not become engaged and married; rather, the story continues with the two dialoguing cautiously and circuitously about life and culture, faith and the Messiah. At the apex of the conversation, the Samaritan woman recognizes Jesus to be the Messiah (John 4:25-26), shares the good news with her village (John 4:28-29), and the villagers too confess that Jesus is "the Savior of the world" (John 4:42 NRSV).

So, a natural marriage does not materialize at the end of this story; but, in a way, the Samaritan woman and Jesus are spiritually wedded. Jesus had offered the woman living water at the well (John 4:10-11), that living water being eternal salvation-relationship (John 4:14). She (along with the town) accepts Jesus as life-giving water, i.e., the source of eternal life (cf. John 7:37-39), in that they believed and received Jesus as the Christ and Savior (John 4:39-42). Therefore, a typological wedding does actualize with Jesus as the groom and believing humanity as the bride (cf. John 20:31).

---

7. Alter, *Art of Biblical Narrative*, 62.

Conclusion

THE PRESENT WORK RESEMBLES, in a sense, a survey of the Bible; yet, it is a panorama presented (and hence viewed) through the lens of a metaphorical—though very real—love story metanarrative. It is hoped that this metaphoric love story angle has brought fresh insight and appreciation for God and the plan of God in Scripture. As the discussion concludes, the five stages of God's love story shall be summarized, and the breadth of Scripture which it comprises underscored; subsequently, a few practical implications are drawn concerning the canonical telling of God's love story.

Summary

The betrothal stage of God's love story was charted from Gen 12 to Exod 13 (ch. 1); in this segment of Scripture, the beginning of God's special relationship with a chosen people is developed. God woos and wins the affections of Abraham and Sarah, and their future generations; further, in God's relational pursuit of a people, a family—a bride, as it were—through whom to bless all the nations of the world, God makes substantial promises to the Hebrew people (Gen 12–50). Consequently, with the promises of land, descendants, and blessings reiterated to subsequent patriarchs and the eventual materialization of the same, trust, affection, and hope are engendered on the part of the Hebrews; moreover, the fulfillment of God's betrothal promises, of which the Hebrews are (immediate) beneficiaries, is tantamount to the reciprocity of covenant relationship in its early, premarital phase. In addition, the LORD God proves to be a better suitor and still deserving of affection and loyalty when doing battle against the gods of Egypt, via the ten plagues (Exod 7–13).

In an auxiliary treatment ("Excursus A"), the bride-price, a practice recorded chiefly in Genesis, is seen to be a crucial element in a suitor's betrothal of his future bride. The greater the bride-price, the more valued and esteemed the wife-to-be is in the eyes of her beloved. In a certain sense, similarly, Jesus pays the greatest, highest bride-price in order to enter marriage (salvation) relationship with his bride (the church): his own life.

The marriage stage of God's love story is present mostly in Exod 14 through Num 13 (ch. 2). The wedding (covenant) ceremony was set at Mt. Sinai; preparations are made, and the rites of covenant are undertaken, including a processional, uttering consent, pledging vows, and performing the signing and notarizing, as it were, of the marriage certificate. Indeed, the Mosaic/Sinaitic Covenant is for all intents and purposes a marriage contract (cf. Prov 2:17; Mal 2:14–15; cf. also Jer 31:32), which aims at being fulfilled lovingly and loyally; and, the specific ways in which this marital covenant was so expressed was through the Israelites (1) worshiping the LORD alone, (2) making no idols, and (3) respecting God's name. Flanked on either end of the wedding ceremony (Exod 19–24), is the figurative elopement to the wedding venue (Exod 14–19) and the sublime plans for married (covenant) life in their home together, the promised land, in the near future (Exod 23; cf. Num 13; see further Joshua-Judges).

In addition, the covenant (vow) renewal ceremony was examined ("Excursus B") to provide a perspective of the longevity of covenant adherence; by rehearsing the marital vows (or covenantal blessings and curses), each generation was affirming what God had originally stipulated for their relationship. This covenant (vow) renewal ceremony is exhibited in the Old Testament by Moses in Deuteronomy, Joshua in Joshua, Josiah in 2 Kings, and potentially Ezra in Nehemiah. Relatedly, the vow renewal ceremony of the new covenant in Christ is effectively the Eucharist, Communion,

Conclusion

the Lord's Supper; the regular engagement—also on a generational scale—of the redeemed with her Savior through the ritual act of breaking bread and partaking in the cup of salvation articulates a commitment to the marital (covenantal) terms.

Within God's love story exists also the unfortunate aspect of Israel's unfaithfulness (ch. 3), which prevails throughout much of the former prophets (Joshua–2 Kings); furthermore, the covenantal disobedience is decried by some of the latter prophets in the metaphorical terms of spiritual adultery (e.g., Hosea, Ezekiel). It is the idolatrous and cultic prostitution practices which makes polytheism tantamount to having an affair with illicit lovers. Sadly, this condition of the heart is first detected even at the wedding ceremony of God and Israel (Exod 32–34). In the face of this unfaithfulness, God remains faithful and pursues his bride, vying repeatedly for the affections and trust of wife Israel; this is evidenced most prominently in the life and ministry of Elijah, King Josiah, and the prophet Hosea. For a time, God's bride renews her commitment to her spouse; however, she is eventually allured away by the gods of her neighbors. Consequently, Israel's covenant unfaithfulness is met with covenantal punishments (curses) in order to alert her of her marital compromise, spiritual complacency, relational apathy—and to beckon her to repent, to return to God.

Associated with the foregoing, excursive reflection is given ("Excursus C") to the fact that any time God enters relationship with humanity, the risk of being hurt in that relationship is enormously steep—basically guaranteed—for, the one party is infinite and holy, while the other is finite and fallen. Even with Adam and Eve, before sin enters the world, God positioned Godself in a vulnerable state allowing the humans to be trusting and believing in God, yet this is violated (Gen 1–3). In his incarnation, Jesus equally risks broken relationship; he—vicariously for humanity—becomes broken through his crucifixion and thence miraculously restored in his resurrection so that Jesus might attribute his perfectly intact relationship with God to those who accept his salvific work for their own salvation.

The nadir of God's love story is, in metaphorical terminology, divorce (Jer 2–3; Isa 50:1); the literal counterpart of which is exile (ch. 4). Exile is the final and ultimate covenantal curse (punishment) inflicted when all other more minor warnings failed to be heeded (cf. 2 Kgs 17, 24–25; Jer 52). Jesus explicates the only provision for divorce is marital unfaithfulness (Matt 19:7–9); and, metaphorically speaking, the longevity of Israel's idolatry, i.e., spiritual adultery, constitutes grounds for divorce. Accordingly, the Old Testament speaks of the breaking and broken natures of the covenant (Isa 24:5; Jer 11:10; Ezek 44:7; Zech 11:10), as well as a forthcoming new covenant, which ostensibly renders the original covenant obsolete (Jer 31–32; Hos 2). Alternatively, the Old Testament speaks of God and Israel being separated and estranged for a time; for, Israel is expelled from the house, or promised land, by God (or God's punishing agent[s]) in the form of exile (cf. Lev 26; Deut 28). Nevertheless, there is also Scripture which attests God's presence with the Israelites in their exile (Ezek 10–11); and, a foretold new covenant all but guarantees the restoration of (marital) relationship. Henceforth, the return to the promised land after the exile (see Isa 43) inspires hope of relational reconciliation (Ezra-Nehemiah).

Ancillary to this dismal stage of God's love story ("Excursus D") is the identification in Scripture of God's figurative wedding (or signet) ring. In the Old Testament it is implied that the Davidic Covenant—which promises (and is evidenced by) the kingship of a descendant of David on the Jerusalem throne—represents a wedding band, God's commitment to the Davidic dynasty; for, in Jer 22 the last Davidic king before the fall of Jerusalem and Judah is figuratively represented as God's wedding ring which is taken off God's finger. The removal of a wedding band signifies exile. After the seventy-year exile of the Judeans, God's figurative wedding ring is placed again on the hand of God's bride (Hag 2); and this represents God's entrusted leadership care of the remnant in the hands of Zerubbabel, a descendant of the last king of Judah (and of David). Moreover, Jesus, the son of David (see, e.g., Matt 1), is the exact imprint (or signet ring) of God (Heb 1:3); and everyone

Conclusion

upon whom Jesus sets his seal of salvation enjoys the ultimate marriage (covenantal) relationship.

In the final stage of God's love story (ch. 5), the (re)marriage of God to Jews and Gentiles is in view—which comprises the entire New Testament. Not only is this a remarriage of the Israelites promised aforetime by God through prophecy regarding a *new* covenant, this is also a marriage—for the first time—which includes Gentiles, the people of whom Abraham's descendants would bless (cf. Rom 1:16). In the New Testament, Jesus is directly and indirectly put forward as bridegroom and his disciples as bride (e.g., Mark 2:19–20; John 3:28–30; cf. Isa 60:10). As such, Jesus facilitates his own wedding, or (new) covenant, ceremony at his Last Supper (e.g., Luke 22)—which resembles in part natural Jewish weddings, insofar as the ordering of blessings and cups of wine are administered. Furthermore, the wedding vow, or covenantal legislation, comprises a singularly focused commitment: "I [Jesus] give you a new commandment, that you love one another. Just as I have loved you, you also should love one another" (John 13:34 NRSV). This marriage may materialize and go into effect by virtue of Jesus dying on the cross—thereby making the bride's remarriage possible through the death of her husband, according to the law (Rom 7:1–6; cf. Deut 22, 24)—and by virtue of Jesus resurrecting from the dead may enjoy (re)new(ed) relationship with his bride: i.e., those who accept his salvation by grace through faith (Eph 2:8–9; Rom 10:9–10). The new covenant people are depicted in the New Testament as the bride of Christ in Revelation too (Rev 21), wherein the union of bridegroom and bride are further typified as an eternal wedding banquet (Rev 19). Thus, such is the culmination of, and invitation into, God's love story (Rev 19:9; 22:17)!

Complementary to the (re)marriage phase of God's love story is the elucidation of the wife-at-the-well biblical type-scene ("Excursus E"). In Genesis and Exodus there are three occurrences of a man (or his representative) meeting his to-be-wife at a well; whether it is between Isaac and Rebekah, Jacob and Rachel, or Moses and Zipporah, fateful meetings and even marital arrangements are made at the well. This biblical type-scene is particularly provocative when considering Jesus' encounter with the Samaritan woman at the well at Sychar, Samaria. Instead of a natural marriage, a spiritual one is set in motion. Jesus offers living water (salvation) and she realizes that Jesus is the Messiah (Savior). Eventually, both she and the townsfolk confess Jesus to be the Savior of the world (John 4:42), which is effectively spiritual marriage—salvation!

Implications

There are many implications which may be derived from the examination of the Bible's coherent and comprehensive love story metaphorical analogy. While just a few ramifications are drawn out presently, these are certainly not exhaustive; the reader is encouraged, therefore, to grapple not only with these issues presented below but also with one's own ruminations from the foregoing presentation. It is hoped that robust relationship with the Triune God is realized by means of how God has revealed God's own intention of and design for relationship, as well as the great lengths that it took for the Triune God to enter salvation-relationship with humankind and enjoy the fullness of everlasting covenantal life together.

First, that God enters into a metaphorical marriage with humanity condones, and even encourages, that humans may enter into marriage relationship. Indeed, while it is not explicitly stated, the events of Gen 2 have oft been taken as a marriage covenant (cf. Matt 19:4–6). Consequently, being married or on the pathway to marriage (i.e., engagement) is a good—and potentially God-honoring—enterprise; for, this is the context wherein the convergence of social, spiritual, and physical intimacy—for which humans were created—may be enjoyed in a God-sanctioned relationship.

Second, that God's love story includes not only joyous seasons but also tragic elements, namely unfaithfulness and divorce on the part of his spouse, is instructive. That Israel's serial extramarital affairs (covenant unfaithfulness) committed against God resulted in God divorcing (exiling) his spouse as a grounded punishment legitimates divorce within the parameters which God has specified

Conclusion

(see Deut 22, 24; Matt 5:31–32). Therefore, for individuals who have been the casualty of marital unfaithfulness or who have been divorced, it is remarkable and poignant that God can relate (to some, metaphorical extent) with divorce, and that humans can relate to God in an analogous way. Furthermore, God in Jesus, as fully-God and fully-human, can and does empathize with our human heartbreak, dysfunction, and carnage due to broken relationship; for "we do not have a high priest who is unable to sympathize with our weaknesses, but we have one who in every respect has been tested as we are, yet without sin" (Heb 4:15 NRSV).

Third, that God remarries the Israelites/Jews is very restorative. Under the right circumstances, it therefore follows that remarriage is something permitted by God. While this is a complex and complicated matter, God is a God of new beginnings, a God of forgiveness and redemption.

In conclusion, it seems axiomatic to say that it is every human's desire to love and to be loved; indeed, this appears to be the by-product of being created in community (male and female [cf. Gen 1–2]) by the Triune God of love. In that vein, therefore, I pronounce a blessing upon you, the reader: May you love well and may you be open to being loved well; moreover, may the Holy Spirit apply the healing of Christ to your whole being, and may the Holy Spirit fortify your resolve to continue or (re)engage in loving relationship with God and with others, thereby living the way of Jesus Christ!

Bibliography

Adams, Jay E. *Marriage, Divorce, and Remarriage in the Bible: A Fresh Look at What Scripture Teaches*. Grand Rapids: Zondervan, 1980.
Albertz, Rainer. *A History of the Israelite Religion in the Old Testament Period*. 2 vols. Translated by John Bowden. OTL. Philadelphia: Westminster John Knox, 1994.
Albright, W. F., and C. S. Mann. *Matthew*. AB. Garden City: Doubleday, 1971.
Alter, Robert. *The Art of Biblical Narrative*. 2nd ed. New York: Basic Books, 2011.
Bar, Shaul. "What Did the Servant Give to Rebecca's Brother and Mother?" *Bib* 94 (2013) 565–72.
Bar-Efrat, Shimon. *Narrative Art in the Bible*. Translated by Dorothea Shefer-Vanson, with Shimon Bar-Efrat. JSOTSup 70. Sheffield: Almond, 1989.
Beale, G. K. *The Book of Revelation: A Commentary on the Greek Text*. NIGTC. Grand Rapids: Eerdmans, 1999.
Birch, Bruce C. "The Moral Trajectory of the Old Testament Drama: Creation, Exodus, Exile." In *Restorative Readings: The Old Testament, Ethics, and Human Dignity*, edited by L. Juliana Claassens and Bruce C. Birch, 3–16. Eugene, OR: Pickwick, 2015.
Bonhoeffer, Dietrich. *The Cost of Discipleship*. Rev. ed. New York: Collier; MacMillan, 1963.
Budge, E. A. Wallis. *Egyptian Religion: Egyptian Ideas of the Future Life*. New York: Gramercy, 1996.
———. *Osiris and the Egyptian Resurrection*. 2 vols. New York: Putnam, 1911.
Carmichael, Deborah Bleicher. "David Daube on the Eucharist and the Passover Seder." *JSNT* 13 (1991) 45–67.
Chambers, Nathan J. "Confirming Joshua as the Interpreter of Israel's Tôrāh: The Narrative Role of Joshua 8:30–35." *BBR* 25 (2015) 141–53.
Childs, Brevard S. *Introduction to the Old Testament as Scripture*. Philadelphia: Fortress, 1989.
———. *Memory and Tradition in Israel*. SBT 37. Naperville, IL: Allenon, 1962.
Collins, Raymond F. "Marriage (NT)." In *ABD* 4:569–72.
Craigie, Peter C. *The Book of Deuteronomy*. NICOT. Grand Rapids: Eerdmans, 1976.

Bibliography

Culley, Robert. *Studies in the Structure of Hebrew Narrative*. SemeiaSup. Philadelphia: Fortress, 1976.

Davies, Eryl W. *Biblical Criticism: A Guide for the Perplexed*. London: Bloomsbury, 2013.

Day, John. "Asherah in the Hebrew Bible and Northwest Semitic Literature." *JBL* 105 (1986) 385–408.

Dever, William G. *Did God Have a Wife? Archaeology and Folk Religion in Ancient Israel*. Grand Rapids: Eerdmans, 2005.

Dozeman, Thomas B. *Joshua 1–12: A New Translation with Introduction and Commentary*. AB. New Haven: Yale University Press, 2015.

Drinkard, Joel F., Jr. "Religious Practices Reflected in the Book of Hosea." *RevExp* 90 (1993) 205–18.

Duggan, Michael W. *The Covenant Renewal in Ezra-Nehemiah (Neh 7:72b–10:40): An Exegetical, Literary, and Theological Study*. SBLDS 164. Atlanta: SBL, 2001.

Dumbrell, William J. *Covenant and Creation: An Old Testament Covenant Theology*. Rev. ed. Milton Keynes: Paternoster, 2013.

Evans, Craig A. *Luke*. NIBC 3. Peabody: Hendrickson, 1990.

Fekkes, Jan, III. "'His Bride Has Prepared Herself': Revelation 19–21 and Isaian Nuptial Imagery." *JBL* 109 (1990) 269–87.

Fensham, F. C. "A Few Observations on the Polarisation between Yahweh and Baal in 1 Kings 17–19." *ZAW* 92 (1980) 227–36.

Fuller, Daniel P. *Gospel and Law: Contrast or Continuum? The Hermeneutics of Dispensationalism and Covenant Theology*. Grand Rapids: Eerdmans, 1980.

Glucksberg, Sam. *Understanding Figurative Language: From Metaphor to Idioms*. OPS 36. Oxford: Oxford University Press, 2001.

Greenberg, Blu. "Marriage in the Jewish Tradition." *JES* 22 (1985) 3–20.

Gutiérrez, Gustavo. *A Theology of Liberation: History, Politics, and Salvation*. New York: Orbis, 1988.

Hamilton, Victor P. "Marriage (OT and ANE)." In *ABD* 4:559–69.

Henriksen, Jan-Olav. "God Revealed through Human Agency: Divine Agency and Embodied Practices of Faith, Hope, and Love." *NZSTh* 58 (2016) 453–72.

Horton, Michael. *Introducing Covenant Theology*. Grand Rapids: Baker, 2006.

House, H. Wayne, ed. *Divorce and Remarriage: Four Christian Views*. Downers Grove: InterVarsity, 1990.

Huber, Lynn R. *Like a Bride Adorned: Reading Metaphor in John's Apocalypse*. ESEC 10. London: T. & T. Clark, 2007.

Hugenberger, Gordon P. *Marriage as a Covenant: A Study of Biblical Law and Ethics Governing Marriage, Developed from the Perspective of Malachi*. VTSup 52. Brill: Leiden, 1994.

Instone-Brewer, David. *Divorce and Remarriage in the Bible: The Social and Literary Context*. Grand Rapids: Eerdmans, 2002.

BIBLIOGRAPHY

Janowiak, Janusz. *"I the Lord Your God Am a Jealous God": A Historical, Exegetical, and Theological Investigation of Divine Zeal and Jealousy in the Old Testament*. Sacra Pagina 2. Rome: Carmelite Editions, 2016.

Janzen, Waldemar. "The First Commandments of the Decalogue and the Battle against Idolatry in the Old Testament." *Vision* 12 (2011) 14–24.

Jeremias, Joachim. *The Eucharistic Words of Jesus*. Translated by Arnold Ehrhardt. Oxford: Blackwell, 1955.

———. *The Parables of Jesus*. Rev. ed. Translated by S. H. Hooke. New York: Scribner, 1963.

———. "νύμφη, νυμφίος." In *TDNT* 4:1099–106.

Jindo, Job Y. *Biblical Metaphor Reconsidered: A Cognitive Approach to Poetic Prophecy in Jeremiah 1–24*. HSM 64. Winona Lake, IN: Eisenbrauns, 2010.

Keller, Timothy. *Generous Justice: How God's Grace Makes Us Just*. New York: Penguin, 2010.

Klein, Jacob. "Sacral Marriage." In *ABD* 5:866–70.

Kline, Meredith G. *Kingdom Prologue: Genesis Foundations for a Covenantal Worldview*. Eugene, OR: Wipf & Stock, 2006.

Kim, Brittany. "Yhwh as Jealous Husband: Abusive Authoritarian or Passionate Protector? A Reexamination of a Prophetic Image." In *Daughter Zion: Her Portrait, Her Response*, edited by Mark J. Boda et al., 127–47. AIIL 13. Atlanta: SBL, 2012.

LaRondelle, Hans K. *Our Creator Redeemer: An Introduction to Biblical Covenant Theology*. Berrien Springs, MI: Andrews University Press, 2005.

Levenson, Jon D. *The Love of God: Divine Gift, Human Gratitude, and Mutual Faithfulness in Judaism*. Princeton: Princeton University Press, 2016.

———. *Resurrection and the Restoration of Israel: The Ultimate Victory of the God of Life*. New Haven: Yale University Press, 2006.

Limburg, James. *Jonah: A Commentary*. OTL. Louisville: Westminster John Knox, 1993.

Magness-Gardiner, Bonnie S. "Seals, Mesopotamian." In *ABD* 5:1062–4.

Marshall, I. Howard. *The Gospel of Luke*. NIGTC. Grand Rapids: Eerdmans, 1978.

Mays, James Luther. *Hosea: A Commentary*. OTL. Philadelphia: Westminster, 1969.

McKnight, Scot. *The Jesus Creed: Loving God, Loving Others*. Brewster, MA: Paraclete, 2004.

Nelson, Richard D. *Joshua: A Commentary*. OTL. Louisville: Westminster John Knox, 1997.

Ortlund, Raymond C., Jr. *God's Unfaithful Wife: A Biblical Theology of Spiritual Adultery*. NSBT 2. Westmont, IL: IVP Academic, 2003.

———. *Marriage and the Mystery of the Gospel*. SSBT. Wheaton, IL: Crossway, 2016.

Pinch, Geraldine. *Handbook of Egyptian Mythology*. Santa Barbara, CA: ABC-CLIO, 2002.

Bibliography

Pitre, Brant. *Jesus the Bridegroom: The Greatest Love Story Ever Told*. New York: Image, 2017.

Reddish, Mitchell G. "Bride of Christ." In *ABD* 1:782.

Rendtorff, Rolf. *The Canonical Hebrew Bible: A Theology of the Old Testament*. Translated by David E. Orton. Leiden: Deo, 2005.

Roberts, Barbara. *Not under Bondage: Biblical Divorce for Abuse, Adultery and Desertion*. Ballarat, Australia: Maschil, 2008.

Roloff, Jürgen. *The Revelation of John*. Translated by John E. Alsup. CC. Minneapolis: Fortress, 1993.

Ruppert, Lothar. "The Foreigner and Association with Foreigners in the Old and New Testaments." Translated by Beth J. Jenkins. *Covenant Quarterly* 55 (1997) 151–63.

Sanders, James A. *Canon and Community: A Guide to Canonical Criticism*. 2nd ed. Eugene, OR: Wipf & Stock, 2000.

Schulz, Regine. "Gods of Ancient Egypt." In *Egypt: The World of the Pharaohs*, edited by Regine Schulz and Matthias Seidel, 522–23. Cologne: Köneman, 1998.

Silverman, Morris, ed. *The Passover Haggadah*. Rev. ed. Bridgeport, CT: Prayer Book, 1975.

Smolarz, Sebastian Ryszard. *Covenant and the Metaphor of Divine Marriage in Biblical Thought: A Study with Special Reference to the Book of Revelation*. Eugene, OR: Wipf & Stock, 2011.

Ska, Jean-Louis. *"Our Fathers Have Told Us": Introduction to the Analysis of Hebrew Narratives*. SB 13. Rome: Pontifical Biblical Institute, 1990.

Spero, Shubert. "'And Against All the Gods of Egypt I Will Execute Judgments...'" *JBQ* 27 (1999) 83–88.

Stienstra, Nelly. *YHWH Is the Husband of His People: Analysis of a Biblical Metaphor with Special Reference to Translation*. Kampen, Netherlands: Kok Pharos, 1993.

Stuart, Douglas K. *Exodus*. NAC 2. Nashville: Broadman & Holman, 2006.

———. *Hosea-Jonah*. 1st ed. WBC 31. Nashville: Nelson, 1987.

Tilford, Nicole L. *Sensing World, Sensing Wisdom: The Cognitive Foundation of Biblical Metaphors*. AIIL 31. Atlanta: SBL, 2017.

Van Seters, John. *Abraham in History and Tradition*. New Haven: Yale University Press, 1975.

Wall, Robert W. "Divorce." In *ABD* 2:217–19.

Waters, Guy Prentiss. *The Lord's Supper as the Sign and Meal of the New Covenant*. SSBT. Wheaton, IL: Crossway, 2019.

Weiss, Andrea L. *Figurative Language in Biblical Prose Narrative: Metaphor in the Book of Samuel*. VTSup 107. Leiden: Brill, 2006.

Weinfeld, Moshe. "Feminine Features in the Imagery of God in Israel: The Sacred Marriage and the Sacred Tree." *VT* 46 (1996) 515–29.

Wenham, Gordon J., and William E. Heth. *Jesus and Divorce*. Rev. ed. Eugene, OR: Wipf & Stock, 2010.

Bibliography

Westermann, Claus. *Genesis 12–36*. Translated by John J. Scullion. CC. Minneapolis: Fortress, 1995.

Whittle, Sarah. *Covenant Renewal and the Consecration of the Gentiles in Romans*. SNTSMS 161. Cambridge: Cambridge University Press, 2015.

Williams, James G. "The Beautiful and the Barren: Conventions in Biblical Type-Scenes." *JSOT* 5 (1980) 107–19.

Woudstra, Marten H. *The Book of Joshua*. NICOT. Grand Rapids: Eerdmans, 1981.

Wright, N. T. *How God Became King: The Forgotten Story of the Gospels*. San Francisco: HarperOne, 2012.

www.ingramcontent.com/pod-product-compliance
Lightning Source LLC
Chambersburg PA
CBHW072156160426
43197CB00012B/2415